MW01078271

Working Across Cultures

MARKET LEADER

Business English

Adrian Pilbeam

PEARSON

Longman

FINANCIAL
TIMES

Pearson Education Limited
Edinburgh Gate
Harlow
Essex CM20 2JE
England
and Associated Companies throughout the world.

www.pearsonlongman.com

© Pearson Education Limited 2010

The right of Adrian Pilbeam to be identified as author of this Work has been asserted by him in accordance with the Copyright, Designs and Patents Act 1988.

All rights reserved; no part of this publication may be reproduced, stored in a retrieval system, or transmitted in any form or by any means, electronic, mechanical, photocopying, recording, or otherwise without the prior written permission of the Publishers.

First published 2010
Fourth impression 2015

ISBN 978-1-408-22003-0

Set in Metaplus, Times & ITC Cheltenham

Printed in Malaysia (CTP-VVP)

Acknowledgements

This series was developed and written by consultants working with LTS Training and Consulting, Bath, a specialist language and intercultural training company.

The author and publishers are grateful to the following teachers who reported on earlier drafts of this material: Aukjen Bosma and Christine Thuillier.

The author would like to thank many colleagues from the SIETAR network in Europe and the US from whom he has gained invaluable insights into the intercultural field over the last 15 years.

We are grateful to the following for permission to reproduce copyright material:

Tables

Table in Unit 12 from 'HSBC Bank International Expat Explorer Survey 08 – Report 2: Offshore Offspring' p3, www.offshore.hsbc.com, copyright © Hill & Knowlton Limited.

Text

Extract from Unit 2 adapted from 'Communicating across the cultural divide', Personnel Today, 22 May 2007, www.personneltoday.com, copyright © *Personnel Today*; Extract from Unit 16 adapted from 'An international outlook: Infosys Trainee Scheme', *The Independent*, 27 September 2007 (Hilpern, K.), copyright © Independent News and Media Limited 2007; Extract from Unit 17 adapted from Leaders' Quest, www.leadersquest.org, granted with permission.

The Financial Times

Extract from Unit 1 adapted from 'Barriers can give a competitive edge', *The Financial Times*, 17 August 2004 (Witzel, M.), copyright © Financial Times Ltd; Extract from Unit 4 adapted from 'Doing business in China: learn from Dell', *The Financial Times*, 11 February 2005 (di Paola, P. and Manning, T.), copyright © Financial Times Ltd; Extract from Unit 6 adapted from 'Case of the "killer elevator"', *The Financial Times*, 19 February 2009 (Tucker, S.), copyright © Financial Times Ltd; Extract from Unit 9 adapted from 'Can the new CEO end a culture clash after a merger?', *The Financial Times*, 10 September 2008, copyright © Financial Times Ltd; Extract from Unit 12 adapted from 'Britain down expat's wish-list for children', *The Financial Times*, 18 September 2008 (Turner, D.), copyright © Financial Times Ltd; Extract from Unit 13 adapted from 'Virtual teams need to build trust', *The Financial Times*, 8 September 2004 (Maitland, A.), copyright © Financial Times Ltd; Extract from Unit 14 adapted from 'A melting pot for forging success', *The Financial Times*, 8 March 2009 (Marsh, P.), copyright © Financial Times Ltd.

In some instances we have been unable to trace the owners of copyright material, and we would appreciate any information that would enable us to do so.

Photos

The publisher would like to thank the following for their kind permission to reproduce their photographs:

(Key: b-bottom; c-centre; l-left; r-right; t-top)

Alamy Images: Barrie Harwood Photography 29tr, Drive Images 5, Eye-Stock 17, idp geneva collection 29l, MARKA 41; **Corbis:** Ralph A. Clevenger 7, moodboard 45; **Getty Images:** AFP 37, Camelot 13, India Today Group 21, 65, Seth Joel 9; **iStockphoto:** 53, 69, 73, Anja Hild 33, Huriye Akinci Iriyari 57, Andrew Rich 49, Agnieszka Szymczak 61; **Jupiter Unlimited:** Comstock Images 25; **Photolibrary.com:** Odilon Dimier 3

All other images © Pearson Education

Every effort has been made to trace the copyright holders and we apologise in advance for any unintentional omissions. We would be pleased to insert the appropriate acknowledgement in any subsequent edition of this publication.

Cover photo © Getty Images: Edouard Berne

Project managed by Chris Hartley

Contents

Overcoming cultural barriers

This unit considers the cultural issues which can arise when a company starts working internationally.

BEFORE YOU READ

Discuss these questions.

1 What are the main reasons for a company to start looking outside its domestic market?
2 What are some of the problems that might arise when marketing and advertising products in different countries?
3 What kind of cultural problems can arise when a company starts working internationally?

READING

A **Understanding the main points**

Read the article on the opposite page and say whether these statements are true (T), false (F) or there is not enough information given (N). Identify the part of the article that gives this information.

1 Most companies only start working internationally when they have fully exploited their domestic market.
2 The best way to enter foreign markets is to set up subsidiaries in those countries.
3 Geert Hofstede was the first person to study the impact of culture on working internationally.
4 Geert Hofstede found that values and beliefs in different parts of IBM across the world were different.
5 The biggest problem when working internationally is getting the marketing right.
6 China is the most difficult foreign country for Western companies to do business in.
7 Cultural diversity can be a benefit as well as a problem.

B **Understanding details**

Read the article again and answer these questions.

1 What is Geert Hofstede's nationality?
2 When did Hofstede carry out his research at IBM?
3 Why was IBM a good company to choose for his research?
4 Why was 'Nova' a bad name for a car in Spanish-speaking markets?
5 Why was the Lexus luxury car less successful in Europe than in the US?
6 What can companies do to be more successful when marketing products internationally?
7 Why do Western companies have problems operating in China?
8 What are some of the benefits of working across cultures?

Barriers can give a competitive edge

by Morgan Witzel

A Sooner or later, the growing company will reach market saturation in its domestic market, and there will be little choice but to move into overseas markets.

B Most companies, in fact, start dipping their toes into foreign waters long before they reach domestic saturation, to exploit other profitable markets and give themselves experience of working abroad.

C Whether the company is trading abroad or establishing foreign subsidiaries, the issue of national culture assumes great importance. It had been known for years that working across cultures poses special problems, but the work of Geert Hofstede, the Dutch management theorist, in the 1970s and 1980s showed just how diverse and various cultural influences can be.

D Working across a single global company – IBM, a business noted for the uniformity of its corporate culture – Hofstede showed that a huge variety of beliefs and values were present in the workplace, not just between the US, Europe and Asia, but within regions as well.

E Globalisation is said to be leading to cultural convergence but, as Hofstede and many later studies have shown, full convergence is still some way away.

F Companies moving into international markets will usually first feel the effects of culture on their marketing and advertising. Every international marketer has their collection of mistakes, where the values of one culture fail to translate into another. Sales of the Vauxhall Nova in Hispanic-speaking countries, for example, suffered because in Spanish, *no va* means 'won't go'.

G Other failures are more complex and based on deeper cultural divides. Toyota's luxury car, the Lexus, was an immediate hit in the US, where the luxury-car market had been the preserve of a few domestic companies, and the Lexus offered something appreciably different. The Lexus has been much less successful in Europe, where there is a stronger tradition of luxury car-making and strong loyalty to local brands on the part of their buyers.

H Cultural barriers in marketing can be overcome by repositioning brands, changing advertising and product features to suit local sensitivities and so on. Much more difficult to manage are the cultural differences that arise when companies establish multinational subsidiaries and then expect members of different national cultures to work together. This is especially the case with Western companies establishing subsidiaries in China.

I Chinese workers often prefer strong, directive leadership to the more democratic model now common in the West. They also rely much more on senior managers to sort out problems, including problems in the workers' private lives. Linguistic confusion is also compounded by quite different attitudes to issues such as ethics, reporting and control, and workers' rights and responsibilities.

J What appears to be a barrier, however, can actually be a source of competitive advantage for those companies and managers that learn to work with cultural differences and benefit from them.

K In terms of managing local subsidiaries, some global companies have learnt to adopt best practices from foreign companies and transfer these into the home market. This kind of cross-fertilisation has been taking place between Japanese and Western car-makers for decades, and has led to powerful innovations on both sides.

FT

VOCABULARY

A Understanding expressions

Choose the best explanation for each phrase from the article.

1 '... will *reach market saturation* ...' (line 2)
   a) start to lose market share
   b) stop expanding its market share

2 '... start *dipping their toes* into foreign waters ...' (lines 6–7)
   a) making the first moves·
   b) carrying out test marketing

3 '... leading to *cultural convergence* ...' (lines 30–31)
   a) where everything becomes similar
   b) where everything changes

4 '... will usually first *feel the effects of culture* on ...' (lines 35–36)
   a) have cultural problems
   b) be influenced by culture

5 '... based on deeper cultural *divides*.' (line 46)
   a) differences
   b) values

6 '... to *suit local sensitivities* ...' (line 61)
   a) adapt to different ways of doing things
   b) try to change the local customs

7 'Linguistic confusion is also *compounded* by ...' (lines 76–77)
   a) made better
   b) made worse

8 '... a source of *competitive advantage* ...' (lines 82–83)
   a) a reason for problems with competitors
   b) a chance to be better than competitors

9 '... to *adopt best practices* from ...' (line 89)
   a) improve by constant practice
   b) take good ideas from others

B Word search

Find words or phrases in the article which fit these meanings.

1 markets in foreign countries (paragraph A)

2 to use fully so you get as much advantage as possible from it (paragraph B)

3 companies that are at least half owned and controlled by another company (paragraph C)

4 causes (a problem) (paragraph C)

5 ideas that you feel to be true (paragraph D)

6 the principles that influence the way of life of a particular group or community (paragraph D)

7 place reserved for one special group (paragraph G)

8 being faithful to a set of beliefs or a country (paragraph G)

9 things that prevent or limit what you can do (paragraph H)

10 changing the way of marketing and advertising a product or a brand so that people think about it in a different way (paragraph H)

11 set up, create (paragraph H)

12 a style of management that shows you are clearly in charge (paragraph I)

13 to solve (paragraph I)

14 the mixing of the ideas of different groups of people, which often produces a better result (paragraph K)

C Sentence completion

Use words and phrases from Exercise B in the correct form to complete these sentences.

1 Multinational companies usually have . . . . in many parts of the world.

2 Some companies are more successful in . . . . markets than in their domestic market.

3 Having a presence in a market is the best way to . . . . it fully.

4 Sometimes it is necessary to . . . . a product or brand in a foreign market in order to avoid offending or confusing people.

5 To sell products successfully in foreign markets, it is usually necessary to . . . . local sales companies.

OVER TO YOU

1 What are the positive aspects of working across cultures?

2 What are the challenges or difficulties of working across cultures?

3 The words in the box are all associated with culture. How would you explain or define each of them?

> artefacts   assumptions   attitudes   behaviour   beliefs
> dress   food   language   norms   traditions   values

4 A common image of culture is that of an iceberg. Look at the photo. Why do you think that is?

5 Which of the words in question 3 associated with culture are above the surface of the iceberg of culture and are clearly visible, and which are below the surface and invisible? For those below the surface, how far below the surface do you think they are? Say why.

6 What are some of the core values in your culture?

7 Some examples are given in the article about brands and products that have not transferred well to overseas markets. Can you think of others?

The iceberg of culture

Communicating across cultures

This unit describes how communication styles differ across cultures.

BEFORE YOU READ

Discuss these questions.

1 In what ways do you think working internationally has changed in recent years?
2 What personal skills and qualities are important if you want to work successfully with people from other cultures?
3 What examples can you think of where differences in communication styles might cause problems when working across cultures?

READING

A Understanding the main points

Read the article on the opposite page and choose the statement that expresses the ideas in the article most accurately.

1 Europeans find it hard to work with people from the Middle East and Asia.
2 You need to adapt your behaviour and communication style when working across cultures.
3 Maintaining group harmony is the most important quality needed by international managers.

B Understanding details

Read the article again and answer these questions.

1 In what ways has the world of work changed in recent years?
2 How are some international software development projects run nowadays?
3 What is the result of increased interaction between colleagues from different countries?
4 What do organisations need in order to be effective in different countries?
5 What research did PDI carry out?
6 How big was PDI's survey?
7 What are 'The Big Five'?
8 What was one of the most important findings from the research?
9 How did managers from the UK score on the research?
10 How did managers from Saudi Arabia and Japan score?
11 What can happen when British managers come into contact with managers from Saudi Arabia or Japan?
12 What is one potential problem when British people work with the Chinese?

Communicating across the cultural divide

A Until quite recently, company leaders who worked closely with foreign colleagues either travelled regularly or were transferred overseas. But the
5 world of work has changed dramatically. Now, many managers regularly interact with foreign clients, vendors or fellow employees without ever leaving their offices.

B For instance, an HR manager in London may, on the same day, talk with a colleague in Asia and a customer in the US. Or a software developer in Dublin can pass on an around-
15 the-clock software project each afternoon to a colleague in California, and get it back the next morning from a colleague in Bangalore.

C This increased interaction with
20 colleagues in other countries can result in a dramatic contrast in styles, cultures and expectations. That, in turn, makes it more important to ensure your organisation has access to the inter-
25 personal and management skills needed to be effective in the countries in which it operates.

D Research from global HR consulting firm Personnel Decisions International
30 (PDI) suggests that there are significant differences in core personality traits between business leaders from different countries.

E PDI examined responses on its
35 global questionnaire from nearly 7,500 managers and executives in more than 500 organisations across 12 countries. The survey looked at 39 specific traits that make up what industrial psych-
40 ologists call 'The Big Five' – emotional balance, extroversion, conscientiousness, agreeableness and openness to new experiences.

F Chief among the research findings
45 is the fact that agreeableness and emotional balance account for the biggest differences between managers and executives working across different countries.

G Business leaders in the UK had among the lowest scores on agreeableness – the tendency to seek group harmony – and received average scores in emotional balance. Executives in
55 the UK, as well as other EU countries including Germany and the Netherlands, scored high on extroversion, meaning they like to work in groups.

H In contrast, managers and executives
60 in countries such as Saudi Arabia and Japan are more concerned about maintaining group harmony, and seem more in touch with their emotions and feelings, but they are less inclined to
65 speak openly.

I Given increased international interaction and big differences in styles and cultures, it is important for you to be able to match your personal and com-
70 munication styles with those of colleagues in other countries.

J 'Without realising it, you may not put as much emphasis on group harmony, so you are at risk of coming
75 across as more abrupt or non-caring to managers in countries such as Japan or Saudi Arabia,' says Simon Callow, Vice-President and Managing Director Director of PDI UK.

K And there are other differences. A brainstorming session is a common exercise in the UK, where open group discussion is accepted. However in China, executives scored low on extro-
85 version, preferring to work on problems alone rather than with others. If you propose a brainstorming session with Chinese colleagues, you could be met with great resistance, mean-
90 ing your effort is likely to be a waste of time.

L To be successful when working across cultures, you need to recognise the differences in cultural behaviours
95 and personality traits so you can learn how to adapt your behaviour and your communication style.

from *Personnel Today*

VOCABULARY

A **Understanding expressions**

1 Match 'The Big Five' personality traits described in the article (1–5) with their definitions (a–e).

1	emotional balance	**a)**	tendency to be original, creative and curious
2	extroversion	**b)**	tendency to be reliable, well-organised, self-disciplined and careful
3	conscientiousness	**c)**	tendency to be sociable, friendly, fun-loving and talkative
4	agreeableness	**d)**	tendency to be calm, relaxed and secure
5	openness to new experiences	**e)**	tendency to be good-natured, sympathetic, forgiving and helpful to others

2 Match each of these statements to one of 'The Big Five' personality traits in Exercise 1.

a) I like to follow a schedule.

b) I have a vivid imagination.

c) I start conversations.

d) I give time to others.

e) I am the life and soul of the party.

f) I don't get upset easily.

g) I pay attention to detail.

h) I am calm, relaxed and at ease most of the time.

i) I am full of ideas.

j) I make people feel at ease.

B **Sentence completion**

Use the words and phrases in the box to complete the sentences.

abrupt   come across   effort   expectations   harmony   inclined
interaction   interpersonal   met with resistance   non-caring   traits

1 If you are unlikely to succeed in doing something, then making an extra .... will probably be a waste of time.

2 If you are too direct and unhelpful to people, you may appear to them to be .... and ....

3 If you are in regular contact with people, that means you have a lot of .... with them.

4 We all have .... and make assumptions about how people will behave before we meet them.

5 People who communicate well with other people usually have good .... skills.

6 .... are qualities that are part of someone's personality.

7 If you do not want to do something, then you are not .... to do it.

8 The impression you make on other people is also how you .... to them.

9 If people really don't want to do what you suggest, then your ideas will probably be ....

10 In Asian cultures, group .... is important, so people do not openly disagree with each other.

C Synonyms

Find words in the article which mean the same as these words.

1 chiefs/bosses   6 24/7

2 fellow employees   7 managers

3 abroad   8 companies

4 customers   9 study

5 suppliers   10 by yourself

D Prepositions

Complete these sentences using the prepositions in the box.

about	at	for	in	of	on	up	with	with

1 Increased contact with colleagues from other countries has resulted .... big contrasts in ways of working and communicating.

2 The PDI survey looked .... personality traits in leaders from different countries.

3 In particular, the study examined the personality traits that make .... 'The Big Five'.

4 Agreeableness and emotional balance account .... the biggest differences between managers from different countries.

5 Managers from Asian and Middle Eastern countries are particularly concerned .... maintaining group harmony.

6 Managers from Asian and Middle Eastern countries are also more in touch .... their emotions and feelings.

7 To be effective as an international manager, it is important to be able to match your communication style .... those of colleagues from other countries.

8 Western managers put less emphasis .... maintaining group harmony.

9 They are therefore at risk .... coming across as abrupt and non-caring to managers from Asia and the Middle East.

OVER TO YOU

1 'The Big Five' personality traits are not primarily intended to compare styles of behaviour and communication in different cultures. Nevertheless, try to position your culture and one other culture you know well against 'The Big Five'.

2 Based on your findings from question 1, what advice would you give to someone from another culture about working effectively with people from your culture? How should they adapt their behaviour and communication style?

3 Work individually and make a list of eight or nine key personal qualities or characteristics which you think would help someone to be successful when working across cultures. Then compare your list with those of two or three other people and try to reach a group consensus.

Working styles in Japan

This unit looks at the differences between Japanese and Western ways of working and communicating.

BEFORE YOU READ

Discuss these questions.

1 From your experience or knowledge, what are typical ways of working and communicating in Japan or other Asian countries you have worked in?
2 How do Asian working styles contrast with Western ways of working?
3 How do you think decisions are taken in Japanese companies?

READING

A **Understanding the main points**

Read the article on the opposite page and answer these questions.

1 Which of these statements best summarises the key message of the article?
   a) Japanese working and communication styles are not efficient for modern business.
   b) Japanese companies are very slow to take decisions.
   c) Western managers in Japan want their Japanese staff to communicate in a more Western way.
2 What is the normal Japanese way of communicating ideas and information?
3 How are decisions usually taken in Japanese companies?

B **Understanding details**

Read the article again and answer these questions.

1 Why is a whiteboard an unusual feature for the office of a Japanese bank's chief executive?
2 What are the five things Federico Sacasa is trying to get his Japanese employees to do when communicating with him and other Westerners?
3 Why are Japanese employees reluctant to discuss things openly with their bosses?
4 Why do Western managers believe that Japanese working practices lead to low productivity?
5 According to Federico Sacasa, what is the difference between consensus decision-making and decision-making by unanimous consent? Which does he prefer and why?
6 What is the difference between the Japanese way of doing things and how Mr Sacasa would like things done?
7 How confident are Western managers that they will succeed in changing Japanese working practices?

Modernising the Japanese way of working

by Michiyo Nakamoto

A The whiteboard on Federico Sacasa's wall in Aozora Bank's Tokyo headquarters is an unusual feature for the office of a Japanese bank's Chief
5 Executive.
B But the words and drawings in red and blue that fill the board represent an exercise in cultural transformation that Mr Sacasa believes is critical to
10 the future of the bank.
C A Nicaraguan who came to Aozora via Bank of America, Mr Sacasa is encouraging Japanese employees to express their views and to engage
15 in brainstorming with their boss. 'I am perfectly happy to have a conversation,' is the message he conveys to puzzled Japanese staff. The whiteboard is there to help them express ideas. 'I
20 am encouraging people to be a little less formal. I don't want a presentation,

I want a discussion of the issues and the logic,' he says.
D Mr Sacasa is one of an increasing
25 number of foreign managers who are trying to transform Japanese companies into efficient and competitive modern organisations. His experiment with the whiteboard reflects a typical challenge:
30 to persuade Japanese staff to communicate openly and understandably to a non-Japanese.
E Such dialogue is vital not only to ensure everyone understands what is
35 going on, but also to ensure transparency among all employees about issues in the organisation. But free, open expression is not a common feature in Japan's rigidly hierarchical
40 corporate culture, in which subordinates are often expected to be seen and not heard.
F At Mitsubishi Fuso Truck and Bus, which came under the control of

45 German company Daimler in 2005, Japanese Fumio Akikawa is coping with the same problem as Mr Sacasa. He must ensure the Daimler and Fuso sides understand each other. 'Japanese
50 staff will often give a long explanation of the matter under discussion rather than express views directly; and the other side has to figure out what they are getting at,' Mr Akikawa says. 'I tell
55 them it's OK, it's an opinion. I challenge my guys to express their views, but for them it is a bit difficult.'
G Western managers are also trying to end such practices as the need for
60 unanimous consent to make a decision, meticulous planning and focus on processes, which they say lead to low productivity. 'There is a lot of meeting before the meeting to make sure there
65 are no surprises,' Mr Sacasa says. 'Consensus decision-making is where everyone gets a chance to voice their views, and someone with authority makes a decision and everyone sup-
70 ports the decision. But in Japan, what you have is "unanimous consent", which means "everyone agrees ... and one person can stop a decision".'
H Japanese respect for each step of the
75 process and for each person's role is commendable, but results in inefficiencies, suggests Mr Sacasa. 'The goal is to do it right the first time, rather than doing it over and over and checking
80 and going through a lot of processes.'
I The cultural issues foreign managers face run wide and deep, and nobody is under any illusions that change can be achieved overnight. But foreign man-
85 agers are sure that the message will get through more widely and change will take place eventually.

VOCABULARY

A **Understanding expressions**

Choose the best explanation for each word or phrase from the article.

1 '... *critical* to the future of the bank.' (lines 9–10)

   a) extremely important
   b) negative

2 'Such dialogue is *vital* ...' (line 33)

   a) essential
   b) life-giving

3 '... *subordinates* are often expected to be seen and not heard.' (lines 40–42)

   a) junior managers
   b) employees at a more junior level

4 '... Fumio Akikawa is *coping with* the same problem ...' (lines 46–47)

   a) experiencing
   b) dealing with

5 '... the other side has *to figure out* ...' (lines 52–53)

   a) draw a diagram
   b) try to understand

6 '... what they *are getting at* ...' (lines 53–54)

   a) means
   b) understands

7 '... the need for *unanimous* consent ...' (lines 59–60)

   a) which everyone agrees with
   b) which everyone enjoys

8 '... *meticulous* planning ...' (line 61)

   a) very slow and relaxed
   b) very detailed and correct

9 '... a chance *to voice* their views ...' (lines 67–68)

   a) to express
   b) to explain

10 'Japanese respect [...] for each person's role is *commendable* ...' (lines 74–76)

   a) impressive
   b) deserves praise

11 '... nobody *is under any illusions* ...' (lines 82–83)

   a) understands everything
   b) believes something that is not true

12 '... the message will *get through* ...' (lines 85–86)

   a) be understood
   b) succeed

13 '... change will take place *eventually*.' (lines 86–87)

   a) possibly
   b) in the end

B **Word partnerships**

Match the verbs (1–6) with the nouns (a–f).

1	to achieve	a)	issues
2	to express	b)	an explanation
3	to have	c)	a decision
4	to give	d)	views/ideas
5	to make/support	e)	a conversation
6	to face	f)	change

C **Word search**

Complete the chart with as many expressions as you can from the article which describe either the Japanese or Western ways of working and communicating.

Japanese style	Western style
• rigidly hierarchical corporate culture • lots of meetings before the main meeting to make sure there are no surprises • subordinates expected to be seen, not heard	• engage in brainstorming • goal is to do it right the first time • employees expected to express their views

OVER TO YOU

1 Do you agree with the opinion expressed by the Western managers quoted in the article that their Japanese colleagues should learn to communicate and make decisions in a more Western way? Should the same approach be taken in other Asian countries, such as China and Korea? Would that make Japanese or other Asian companies more modern, efficient and competitive?

2 In spite of the suggestion in the article that the Japanese way of working is inefficient, Japanese companies revolutionised the manufacturing process in the 1970s and 1980s, inventing methods such as *kaizen* (continuous improvement), quality circles and the Toyota Production System (which is now known as *lean manufacturing*). What aspects of Japanese culture do you think led to the development of these concepts?

3 How would you describe the typical communication style in your culture, especially between bosses and subordinates? Some examples of communication styles are:

   • direct / indirect
   • explicit / implicit
   • serious / humorous
   • formal / informal
   • serious / friendly

4 Choose another culture you know well. How would you describe the communication style in that culture? How does it differ from the communication style in your culture?

5 In general, do you think foreign managers should impose their own cultural style and way of working on employees in a local subsidiary? Or should they adapt to the local style?

Doing business in China

This unit looks at the steps companies need to take to be successful when entering a foreign market.

BEFORE YOU READ

Discuss these questions.

1   What are some typical mistakes that a company can make when entering a foreign market with a business model from its home market?

2   Can you think of any examples of where a company's entry into a foreign market failed and led to withdrawal from the country?

3   Can you think of any examples where a company has been very successful in entering a foreign market?

READING

A   **Understanding the main points**

Read the article on the opposite page and answer these questions.

1   Which of these statements best summarises the key message of the article?

   a) China is a very difficult market for foreign companies to succeed in.
   b) Designing a new business model specially for the Chinese market is the best way to succeed.
   c) Adapting an existing business model to the Chinese context gives the best chance of success.

2   What was Dell's strategy for the Chinese market?

3   How successful has it been?

B   **Understanding details**

Read the article again and answer these questions.

1   In what ways are Marco Polo's experiences in China relevant today?

2   When did Dell enter the Chinese market?

3   What were the advantages for Dell of adapting its US business model to the Chinese market?

4   What particular aspect of operating in China makes it difficult for companies to plan?

5   What are the two main mistakes a company can make when entering a foreign market like China?

6   What part of Dell's business model did the company introduce in China?

7   How did they need to adapt their business model to suit the particularities of the local market?

8   What is the biggest danger when a company enters a foreign market?

9   Who runs Dell's activities in China now?

Doing business in China: learn from Dell

by Paul DiPaola and Tom Manning

A Of all the business innovations explorer Marco Polo discovered in 13th-century China, he was perhaps most surprised by the use of paper 5 money. It was worth dozens of times the weight of the heavy coins that European traders carried around. Today's multinational technology companies could learn a similar 10 lesson: bring only what's needed when entering China.

B That's what Dell did under Phil Kelly, Dell Asia Pacific's first senior executive. In 1998, he introduced just a 15 part of Dell's famous business model to the Chinese marketplace, adding capabilities and staff as growth dictated. As a result, Dell's share of the PC market grew more than 60 per cent a year 20 between 2000 and 2005, and is forecast to grow at twice the rate of China's overall PC market, giving the company a strong follower position behind IBM/Lenovo.

C The strategy allowed the company to mitigate the risks of trying to force-fit its model to China or abandoning its valuable experience, two common pitfalls for multinationals. It also allowed 30 the company to localise operations, cement relationships with customers and government officials, and control costs in ways that account for the country's often unpredictable rules and 35 opportunities. It's a process that continues today under the leadership of Foo Piau Phang.

D Dell's approach is worth studying. Companies that want to import 40 their business model from their home market are following a natural instinct: they believe they will succeed by continuing to do what they do well. In theory, the company's core 45 capabilities and values would all transfer as a package. Managers would simply adjust downward to satisfy local requirements.

E Alternatively, companies that invest 50 in a new business model for China are responding to what they see as unique conditions. They often begin with an initial arrangement that's very different from their traditional one. Once again, 55 managers intend to incorporate their best capabilities whenever such standardisation would not diminish the customised model for China.

F Unfortunately, importing a comp-60 any's complete business model generally means importing costs as well. Doing things the old way often costs too much in China. But customisation can result in a nearly similar outcome, 65 because so much efficiency is lost through the abandonment of a well-proven model.

G In Dell's case, Mr Kelly and his team roughed out the basics of the business 70 model. There was never any doubt it would be based on the US model. But they used a simpler form of it – 'about 35–40 per cent worth,' Mr Kelly recalls. At first, this meant that Dell 75 sold only a limited line of products – desktops – emphasising corporate buyers. Dell then built call centres and sales teams, but in a way that was focused on the initial target market.

H Mr Kelly had to adjust the model to accommodate local idiosyncrasies, a challenge that continued well beyond his tenure. For instance, even though eligible customers could order PCs 85 online or via phone, low credit-card penetration meant that most were unable to pay with credit cards. Dell created a flexible model that allowed customers to pay on delivery.

I The larger lesson is that business models must be adapted thoughtfully to the Chinese context. The key thing to watch out for is cost. If the business model can only be executed at high 95 cost, the company is probably importing too much of the model and needs to consider possible adjustments. Reducing the model to its core elements, then adding back local pieces over time, 100 allows companies to carefully build on experience.

FT

VOCABULARY

A **Understanding expressions**

Choose the best explanation for each phrase from the article.

1 '*It was worth dozens of times the weight* of the heavy coins ...' (lines 5–6)

   a) it was much more valuable

   b) it was much heavier

2 '... adding capabilities and staff *as growth dictated*.' (lines 16–17)

   a) based on the development of sales

   b) according to the commands of Dell's head office in the US

3 '... giving the company *a strong follower position* ...' (lines 22–23)

   a) a good position in the market

   b) number two in the market

4 '... allowed the company *to mitigate* the risks ...' (lines 25–26)

   a) to reduce the risks

   b) to eliminate the risks

5 '... trying *to force-fit its model to China* ...' (lines 26–27)

   a) to put a lot of effort into making its model work in China

   b) to impose its model on the Chinese market

6 '... two common *pitfalls* for multinationals.' (lines 28–29)

   a) strategies

   b) mistakes

7 '... *cement relationships* with customers and government officials ...' (lines 31–32)

   a) build relationships

   b) strengthen relationships

8 'Managers would simply *adjust downward* to satisfy local requirements.' (lines 46–48)

   a) make small changes to their business model

   b) reduce the quality of their product

9 '... through the *abandonment of a well-proven model*.' (lines 66–67)

   a) not using a model that has not been tested properly

   b) not using a model that has worked many times before

10 '... *roughed out the basics* of the business model.' (lines 69–70)

   a) had a lot of problems at the beginning

   b) did an outline plan at the beginning

11 '... adjust the model *to accommodate local idiosyncrasies* ...' (lines 80–81)

   a) to provide housing for local staff

   b) to adapt to sometimes strange local conditions

B **Word search**

Find words in the article which fit these meanings.

1 the ability of an organisation to do something, especially something difficult (paragraph B)

c........

2 to adapt to the area (paragraph C)

l........

3 behaving in a way you don't expect (paragraph C)

υ........

4 the central or most important part (paragraph D)

c........

5 to add or include something as part of something else (paragraph E)

i........

6 to make something less important or effective (paragraph E)

d........

7 the period of time when someone has an important job (paragraph H)

t........

8 allowed by rules to do something (paragraph H)

e........

9 small changes made to a plan or system (paragraph I)

a........

C **Prepositions**

Match the verbs (1–9) with the prepositions (a–i).

1	to be adapted	**a)**	on
2	to be based	**b)**	out
3	to account	**c)**	on
4	to respond	**d)**	in
5	to arrive	**e)**	for
6	to result	**f)**	to
7	to build	**g)**	to
8	to rough	**h)**	on
9	to be focused	**i)**	at

OVER TO YOU

1 To what extent do you agree with the writers of the article that it is wrong both to import the whole of an existing business model and to develop a completely new model for a new market?

2 Think of some well-known foreign companies that have set up operations in your country, e.g. a retail chain or a restaurant chain. How successful have they been? To what extent have they adapted their business model to suit the local market? Have there been any big failures?

Keeping employees happy in India

This unit looks at how Cisco, a US IT company, plans to attract and keep Indian employees.

BEFORE YOU READ

Discuss these questions.

1 So many Western companies have outsourced operations to India that there is now a shortage of trained IT specialists in India. How can companies attract and keep the best talent?

2 What are the best ways to attract and keep talented and skilled employees in Western countries?

READING

A **Understanding the main points**

Read the article on the opposite page and answer these questions.

1 What is special about the campus Cisco is building in Bangalore?

2 What will be the role of Cisco's new Indian campus in its global operations?

3 Why is Cisco including so many sports and other facilities?

B **Searching for facts and figures**

Read the article again and complete the chart.

Cost of Cisco's new campus	.............................[1]
Size of Cisco's new campus	.............................[2]
Date of opening of the new campus	.............................[3]
Number of employees at the new campus	
• at the start	.............................[4]
• at capacity	.............................[5]
Amount Cisco plans to invest in India	.............................[6]
Percentage of Cisco top executives who will be based in India	.............................[7]
Number of executives from the US, Europe and Singapore currently based in India	.............................[8]
Staff turnover rates at Cisco in India	.............................[9]
Staff turnover rates at competitor companies in India	.............................[10]
Spending planned on R&D by 2010	.............................[11]
Spending planned on sales and marketing by 2010	.............................[12]
Spending planned on its equipment leasing business	.............................[13]

How Cisco plans to attract the local talent

by Amy Yee

A At Cisco's new $50m, 14-acre campus in Bangalore, the cricket pitch is not quite finished. Cranes and trucks move back and forth, and not far from the basketball courts, the aerobics and yoga rooms are still being completed.

B Cisco Globalisation Centre East, as Cisco's largest research-and-design centre outside the US is called, opened at the end of 2007 in India's southern technology hub. Soon after opening, the elegant main building already housed 1,000 employees, and the number will grow to 10,000 in 2011.

C As part of its $1.1bn investment in India, Cisco will base one-fifth of its top executives in India over the next few years as it targets growing markets in the region.

D About 20 executives have already relocated to Bangalore from the US, Europe and Singapore, including Wim Elfrink, Cisco's Chief Globalisation Officer, formerly based at Cisco's headquarters in San Jose, California.

E The amenities seem more suitable for a resort than for offices of the world's largest maker of networking equipment and routers. But in India's talent war, a state-of-the-art campus is critical to attracting top engineers and technologists.

F Although Cisco has low attrition rates of 8 to 9 per cent compared with double-digit rates at other companies, retaining employees is a challenge as opportunities in India grow, and people hop from job to job.

G Hence Cisco insists its efforts are not frivolous. The amenities 'are a must', says Syed Hoda, Chief of Staff at Cisco in Bangalore, as he shows a visitor a multi-cuisine cafeteria equipped with wall projectors for presentations, and a 'break out' room furnished with fashionable modular chairs and shelves of cookie jars.

H Cisco is betting on India as its eastern hemisphere hub, with Bangalore a short flight from the world's leading emerging markets in Asia and the Middle East. 'We want to replicate work here, not shift work,' says Varghese Thomas, Cisco spokesman in Bangalore. 'We want to serve customers directly from here.' To support its plans, Cisco intends to spend more than $750m on research and development by 2010, as well as $100m on sales and marketing and $150m on Cisco Capital, an equipment leasing business.

I Cisco is also diversifying into new applications for networks, such as smart and green buildings. It hopes to use India as a beachhead to take advantage of a massive construction boom in the region, particularly in the Middle East, where new buildings will require cutting-edge technology.

J Retail is also a growth area for Cisco, which predicts the use of technology such as RFID (radio frequency identification) and is positioning itself for the expansion of regional retail markets.

K Adjacent to the lobby in Cisco's main building, construction workers put the finishing touches to some bright displays. This is a showroom for high-tech systems, as the Bangalore campus is among only a handful of sites outside the US where clients can view these important demonstrations.

C **Understanding details**

Read the article again and say whether these statements are true (T), false (F) or there is not enough information given (N). Identify the part of the article that gives this information.

1 The Cisco campus will have facilities for more than 10 different sports and leisure activities.

2 Cisco's Bangalore campus is the company's largest research centre in the world.

3 Cisco is more successful than many other IT companies in India at keeping employees.

4 The Bangalore campus will service mainly the Indian market.

5 Cisco plans to outsource up to 50 per cent of the work currently done in the US and Europe to Bangalore.

VOCABULARY

A **Definitions**

Match the words and phrases in the box with the definitions below.

> amenities   attrition   beachhead   frivolous   hub   to base   to diversify
> to hop   to position yourself   to put the finishing touches to   to relocate
> to replicate   to retain   to shift   to target

1   the rate at which employees leave a company
2   to do or make something again in exactly the same way
3   to finish the last parts (of a building project)
4   to aim for
5   to put a number of employees in one place
6   to move from one city or country to another for work reasons
7   to move something from one place to another
8   lacking any real purpose; not serious or sensible
9   facilities, things you can use when you visit a place to make your stay more enjoyable
10   to move into new areas of business
11   to move quickly from one job to another
12   a place in the front line from which to launch attacks (usually a military term)
13   to get into the right place so you are ready for the next event
14   the central part of a system that all other parts are connected to
15   to keep people

B **Sentence completion**

Use words and phrases from Exercise A in the correct form to complete these sentences.

1   The shortage of IT graduates in India means that most IT companies have high .... rates.
2   The sports facilities and other .... at the Bangalore campus are designed to attract and .... employees.
3   Cisco's aim is to make its Bangalore campus its .... for getting into markets across South-East Asia and the Middle East.
4   The company has already .... about 20 of its executives to Bangalore.
5   Over the next few years, one-fifth of Cisco's top executives will be .... in Bangalore.
6   Cisco's aim is not to .... work from other parts of the world, but to .... work done elsewhere.
7   Cisco is already .... into new areas of business and is .... itself for new opportunities in the region.
8   Cisco has built its Bangalore campus so that it can .... new markets in South-East Asia.
9   Because of the growth in IT and other outsourcing jobs in India, well-qualified employees .... from job to job quite frequently.
10   Cisco intends to make Bangalore a .... for its activities in Asia and the Middle East.
11   Some people might consider the Cisco campus with all its amenities to be rather .... for a serious IT company.
12   On all building projects, ... things always happens at the last minute.

C   Prepositions

Complete these sentences using the correct prepositions.

1   The aerobics room is adjacent .... the yoga room.

2   Cisco plans to invest a large amount of money .... India.

3   One-fifth of Cisco's top executives will be based .... Bangalore.

4   Cisco has diversified .... RFID technology for the retail industry.

5   Cisco is betting .... India being a key regional centre in the next decade.

6   Cisco has already relocated about 20 of its executives .... Bangalore.

7   Offering a very modern work environment is critical .... attracting the best talent.

8   Cisco plans to use India as a base to take advantage .... the construction boom in the Middle East.

D   Opposites

Find words or phrases from the article which mean the opposite of these.

1   smallest (paragraph B)

2   ugly (paragraph B)

3   shrinking (paragraph C)

4   out-of-date (paragraph E)

5   high (paragraph F)

6   dismissing (paragraph F)

7   serious (paragraph G)

8   tiny (paragraph I)

9   old-fashioned (paragraph I)

10 contraction (paragraph J)

OVER TO YOU

1   Imagine you are members of the management team of Cisco in India. Prepare a presentation to convince the Cisco top management in the US of the need to invest in a new state-of-the-art campus in Bangalore, complete with sports and leisure facilities. Include a description of the state of the labour market, the kind of amenities you think will be necessary, the benefits to Cisco's reputation, etc.

2   How do you see the future trend of outsourcing to India and similar low-cost countries? Will it continue to increase? Will the nature of the work being outsourced change?

This unit looks at the serious problems that can arise when a company is operating in a foreign country and fails to understand the local culture.

BEFORE YOU READ

Discuss these questions.

1 In your own country, what action should a company take if one of its products is found to be faulty and may cause injury to users?

2 If a company's products are found to be faulty in Japan, how do you think the company should react?

READING

A Understanding the main points

Read the article on the opposite page and answer these questions.

1 Which of these statements best summarises the main idea in the article?
  a) The way a company responds to product failure or problems needs to be adjusted to the local cultural norms and expectations.
  b) If a company wants to sell its products on the Japanese market, it needs to make sure that the products are as technically perfect as possible.
  c) Japanese consumers prefer products made in Japan.

2 Why is the Japanese delegation visiting Hong Kong?

3 Was Schindler eventually proved to be at fault for the elevator malfunction?

4 Why did Schindler executives not apologise for the accident immediately?

5 Why does Japanese society expect executives to apologise for mistakes made by their company?

6 What lesson has Schindler learnt from this incident?

B Understanding details

Read the article again and answer these questions.

1 Why has Hong Kong's International Commercial Centre been chosen for the visit by the Japanese group?

2 In which country is Schindler based?

3 Where and when did the accident with the elevator happen?

4 How was the maintenance of the elevator handled?

5 What has the family of the dead teenager decided to do?

6 How did Schindler executives react immediately after the accident?

7 Has Schindler apologised for the accident and the death of the teenager?

8 How does the case of Mitsubishi Fuso compare to Schindler's case?

9 Why are journalists who report on social issues important in this case?

Case of the 'killer elevator'

by Sundeep Tucker

A The sight of a group of Japanese in suits on a recent visit to Hong Kong's International Commerce Centre is striking. Even stranger, the group has
5 not come to admire the stunning views across Victoria Harbour, but to experience the state-of-the-art elevators.

B They are here to see the latest equipment of Schindler, one of the world's
10 leading elevator suppliers. But they have also been invited to Hong Kong by the Switzerland-listed company as part of an attempt to rebuild its image in Japan after the apparent malfunction
15 of one of its elevators resulted in a teenager's death.

C 'We want to show that we are not bad guys,' says Alfred Schindler, Chairman of Schindler Holdings. The
20 company has struggled to sell its elevators and escalators in Japan since the incident in June 2006 in a Tokyo housing complex.

D The company, which denies res-
25 ponsibility for the incident, remains under police investigation. The teenager's family has started legal action against Schindler and at least two unconnected maintenance providers
30 who serviced the elevator after March 2005.

E Japanese public opinion was inflamed by a series of mistakes in the days after the death, when Schindler
35 decided not to co-operate fully with local investigators, or even offer apologies, until it had identified the cause of the malfunction. Since then, it has received not one elevator order,
40 although it has since apologised often.

F The lack of an immediate apology constituted a gross misjudgement in a culture in which corporate executives are expected to apologise quickly
45 and argue about fault later. In Japan, showing remorse is not taken as a legal admission of guilt, as in the West.

G 'The mass media and public took the Schindler response as cold and
50 repugnant ... and the "killer elevator" image was established,' says Professor Nobuo Gohara, of the Center of Corporate Compliance at Toin Yokohama University.

H Professor Gohara says the 'Schindler bashing' of the past two years was due to several factors, not least its inadequate decision-making process and its lack of appreciation of a company's social
60 responsibility in Japanese society.

I Apologies may have been offered, but what are Schindler's chances of redemption? Jochen Legewie, Head of the Toyko office of CNC, a PR consul-
65 tancy, has experience of helping rebuild corporate reputations in Japan. He says any company in a situation such as Schindler's will have to perform many 'purification rituals' to show it is a
70 model corporate citizen.

J He acted for Mitsubishi Fuso, a leading truck maker majority owned by Germany's Daimler, when public anger arose over deaths and injuries linked
75 to faulty parts in 2005. In that case, the truck maker took extensive measures to display remorse. Wilfried Porth, the unit's President, even publicly visited a cemetery to lay flowers.

K Another important step for Schindler will be to focus on gaining the support of journalists who cover social issues rather than technical and business subjects. Only when Schindler
85 has re-established its reputation in the social press can it hope for fair coverage from the business and political media.

L Meanwhile, the company has learnt
90 a hard lesson about operating in a different culture from its own. As Mr Schindler observes: 'Genetically, Westerners are pre-programmed not to apologise unless you are guilty.'

FT

VOCABULARY

A **Understanding expressions**

Choose the best explanation for each phrase from the article.

1 'The company has *struggled* to sell its elevators ...' (lines 19–21)

   a) made a lot of effort
   b) found it difficult

2 '*Japanese public opinion was inflamed* ...' (lines 32–33)

   a) The Japanese public became very angry.
   b) The Japanese public became very sad.

3 'The lack of an immediate apology *constituted a gross misjudgement* ...' (lines 41–42)

   a) caused the company to commit a criminal offence
   b) was a big mistake

4 '... *showing remorse is not taken as a legal admission of guilt* ...' (lines 46–47)

   a) Apologising is not the same as admitting liability.
   b) If a company apologises, they will be forgiven.

5 'The mass media and public *took the Schindler response as cold and repugnant* ...' (lines 48–50)

   a) The media and the public were angry with Schindler.
   b) Schindler's action gave the impression that the company had no sympathy for the death of the teenager.

6 '... the "*Schindler bashing*" of the past two years ...' (lines 55–56)

   a) strong criticism of Schindler
   b) legal cases taken out against Schindler

7 '... *not least its inadequate decision-making process* ...' (lines 57–58)

   a) One of Schindler's most important mistakes was not to take a decision fast enough.
   b) The least important mistake was that it took Schindler a long time to take a decision.

8 '... *what are Schindler's chances of redemption?*' (lines 62–63)

   a) How easy will it be for Schindler to start to make money again in Japan?
   b) How easy will it be for Schindler to restore its good name?

9 '... any company in a situation such as Schindler's will have to *perform many "purification rituals"* to show ...' (lines 67–69)

   a) make sure that it operates in an honest way in future
   b) give public examples to show that it is sorry

10 '... *the company has learnt a hard lesson about operating in a different culture from its own.*' (lines 89–91)

   a) Schindler has found it difficult to learn how to operate in Japan.
   b) It cost Schindler a lot to learn how to operate in Japan.

B **Word search**

Find words or phrases from the article which fit these meanings.

1 extremely modern, with all the latest technology (paragraph A)

s........- o........- t........- a........

2 one of the best in its field (paragraph B)

l........

3 restore its good name (paragraph B)

r........ its i........

4 faulty operation (paragraph B)

m........

5 refuses to accept that it was at fault (paragraph D)

d........ r........

6 a process through the law courts (paragraph D)

l........ a........

7 the important role that a company plays in society (paragraph H)

s........ r........

8 company that fully accepts its responsibilities to society (paragraph I)

m........ c........ c........

9 the opinion people have about how good or bad someone is (paragraph I)

r........

10 automatically made to think or act in a particular way (paragraph L)

p........- p........

OVER TO YOU

1 Imagine you work for a PR consultancy, specialising in communication for crisis management. Schindler executives call you immediately after the elevator accident. They want your advice on what action they should take and how they should communicate with the media. Discuss your ideas and prepare a presentation to give to your client.

2 Do you remember some of these cases of faulty products? How did the companies react? Do you know what effect it had on their sales and their reputation?

- Perrier's bottled mineral water was found to be contaminated with benzene in the US and later in Denmark and the Netherlands.
- Tyres produced by US tyre manufacturer Firestone and fitted on Ford Explorer vehicles were thought to be the cause of accidents.
- Some laptop computer batteries made by Sony caught fire.
- Toys sold by US toy manufacturer Mattel were found to contain traces of lead.

Can you think of any other examples?

3 Based on the information in the article and on your own knowledge and experience, what are some of the important cultural values in Japanese society? What recommendations would you give to Western companies doing business in Japan?

Why international mergers often fail

trickle down effect.

This unit looks at the benefits and difficulties of making international mergers work.

Discuss these questions.

1 Why do companies merge? What do they hope to achieve?
2 What are the typical things that go wrong in mergers and acquisitions?
3 What can companies do to try to ensure success in international mergers?
4 How can you measure whether a merger has been successful?

READING

A **Understanding the main points**

Read the article on the opposite page and say whether these statements are true (T) or false (F).

1 Most mergers succeed in cutting costs and increasing profits.
2 Only a very small percentage of mergers actually achieve their aims.
3 Successful mergers have clear aims from the beginning.
4 Mergers of two competitors are the most likely to succeed.
5 A big problem with international mergers is failure to integrate different working practices.
6 HP's merger with Scitex brought together two very different ways of working.
7 Most international mergers succeed in adding value.
8 Mergers often happen when one partner is not doing well.
9 The main measure of success in a merger is whether the merger has added value.

B **Understanding details**

Read the article again and answer these questions.

1 What are three of the main reasons for mergers and acquisitions?
2 What percentage of mergers are not completely successful in achieving their aims?
3 Why are there plenty of opportunities for things to go wrong in mergers and acquisitions?
4 What is a 'best-of-breed' merger?
5 What advice does Carolyn Firstbrook of Accenture give that might help mergers succeed?
6 How is Scitex's company culture described?
7 What can happen when there is a bad fit between corporate cultures?
8 How did HP manage its acquisition of Scitex?
9 In what ways can cultural differences between merger partners be a good thing?
10 What is the best way of measuring if a merger has been successful?

The art of joining different cultures

by Kim Thomas

A Mergers and acquisitions (M&As) provide a first-class opportunity to cut costs, increase profits and benefit from another company's knowledge and
5 expertise. Yet surveys consistently show that a high proportion of M&As do not fulfil their objectives. One study of senior business leaders conducted by the Hay Group found that only
10 9 per cent of mergers were judged 'completely successful' in achieving their aims. So what goes wrong?

B Studies have found that three conditions are present when M&As take
15 place: that it is not business as usual; there are tight timeframes, with no slack in the system; and that the people making the decisions are biased in a particular direction. These pro-
20 vide plenty of opportunity for things to go wrong.

C Faced with those conditions, it is essential to have strong governance and clear aims. The most successful deals are very clear about the primary
25 goal. Is this about cutting costs through economies of scale? Is it about acquiring a specific capability or product and leveraging that through your
30 existing channels?

D The hardest kind of deal is the 'best-of-breed' merger with a competitor, which means bringing together two powerful management teams, merging
35 two sets of IT systems and aligning two sets of working practices.

E Carolyn Firstbrook, European Head of Strategy at Accenture, the consultancy, maintains that setting clear
40 targets is crucial, and emphasises the importance of managing a tight process as well as taking important decisions quickly.

F Another frequent cause of failure,
45 says Ms Firstbrook, is to under-estimate the cultural difficulties in integrating two companies with very different working practices. When Hewlett-Packard (HP) acquired Scitex, a digital
50 printer company based in Israel with 500 staff, it was taking over an organisation unused to big corporate practices.

G 'You're telling a fairly small, agile company, which doesn't invest a lot
55 in processes or long-term planning, that they need to conform with necessary corporate processes that are totally alien to their culture,' says Pau Molinas, Operations Director for HP's
60 graphics and imaging business.

H The danger is that morale will sink and people will leave the acquired organisation. In fact, says Mr Molinas, in the first 18 months after the acquisi-
65 tion, only four of Scitex's staff have departed. Partly, he says, this was down to the goodwill HP had already established in its acquisition of another Israeli firm, and partly it was due to the
70 hands-off approach HP took towards Scitex: 'It was a market HP didn't have a lot of experience in. We wanted them to have a lot of freedom when it came to investment decisions. So they were
75 teaching us, and they appreciated that.'

I Cultural differences can even add value, says Ms Firstbrook. 'A merger offers a window of opportunity,' she explains, 'when all employees are
80 expecting and prepared for change, to introduce new ways of working that neither side may have accepted in the past.'

J But in the end, the trickiest question
85 is: how do you know whether the merger or acquisition has been successful? Although many deals have disappointing results, it has to be remembered that a merger often hap-
90 pens when at least one party is already doing badly. Ideally, if you want to know if the deal is a success you should be measuring the business value compared to what would have happened if
95 you hadn't done the deal.

FT

VOCABULARY

A Word search

Find words or phrases in the article which fit these meanings.

1 special skills or knowledge that you learn by experience or training (paragraph A)
2 when there is only just enough time (paragraph B)
3 flexibility, room to move or adjust (paragraph B)
4 judging something unfairly because of personal opinions (paragraph B)
5 when making things in larger quantities makes it cheaper to produce each piece (paragraph C)
6 getting as much advantage or profit as possible from something (paragraph C)
7 arranging something so that it is in a similar position to something else (paragraph D)
8 to think that something is smaller or less important than it is (paragraph F)
9 able to move quickly and easily (paragraph G)
10 very different and strange (paragraph G)
11 level of confidence and hope for the future (paragraph H)
12 not interfering or getting too close (paragraph H)
13 most difficult to deal with (paragraph J)

B Word partnerships

Find verbs in the article which go with these nouns.

1 .... costs
2 .... profits
3 .... objectives
4 .... a study
5 .... targets
6 .... decisions
7 .... an organisation
8 .... goodwill
9 .... value
10 .... a deal

C Vocabulary development

Make new word partnerships with the same meanings as those in Exercise B by combining these verbs with nouns from Exercise B.

1 carry out *a study*
2 make ....
3 reduce ....
4 meet ....
5 create ....

6 fix ....
7 conclude ....
8 improve ....
9 raise ....
10 acquire ....

D **Sentence completion**

Use word partnerships from Exercises B and C in the correct form to complete these sentences.

1 A lot of *studies* have been *carried out / conducted* into why mergers often fail to deliver what they promise.

2 The main measure of a successful merger is whether the deal has ....

3 The first step after a merger is usually to look for ways of saving money by ....

4 A longer-term aim, once the merger integration has been completed, is to ...., in order to keep shareholders happy.

5 For some CEOs, ... the .... seems more important than making the merger work.

6 If a merger process is done carefully and sensitively, it can .... a lot of ....

7 Many mergers fail to .... their ....

8 In order to know whether a merger or acquisition has been successful, it is important to .... clear .... against which to measure results.

9 Studies show that it is important to .... clear and quick .... in the early stages of the merger.

10 One of the biggest challenges after .... is integrating two different sets of working practices.

OVER TO YOU

1 A study carried out by the management consulting firm AT Kearney revealed that three main types of mergers and acquisition account for over 90 per cent of all mergers and acquisitions worldwide. Match each merger type (1–3) to its description (a–c).

  1 Volume extension   2 Regional extension   3 Product extension

  a) Merger of non-competitors that serve the same customers with different products and services. The objective is to complement the portfolio and cross-sell products and services.

  b) Merger of direct competitors to increase market share and achieve economies of scale.

  c) Merger of companies in the same industry, but serving different regions. The merging companies want to gain quick access to new geographic segments and local know-how or to increase global market share.

2 Fit these well-known mergers and acquisitions into one of the three categories in question 1.

  a) Arcelor (Luxembourg/France) and Mittal Steel (India)

  b) Renault (France) and Nissan (Japan)

  c) Pepsi Co and Quaker Oats (both US)

  d) Alcatel (France) and Lucent (US)

  e) Daimler (Germany) and Chrysler (US)

  f) Carrefour and Promodes (both France)

  g) Air France (France) and KLM (Netherlands)

  h) Wertkauf (Germany) and Wal-Mart (US)

  Can you think of any other examples?

3 From what you know, which of these mergers have been successful and which not? Why?

Making an international merger work

This unit looks at how a French and a German company managed their merger integration process.

BEFORE YOU READ

Discuss these questions.

1   What are some of the likely cultural problems in international or cross-border mergers?
2   What are some of the fears employees may have after a cross-border merger?
3   Which do you think play a bigger part in cross-border mergers – national culture differences or corporate culture differences?

READING

A   **Understanding the main points**

Read the article on the opposite page and answer these questions.

1   Which companies actually merged?
2   What did the management team do to make sure the merger worked smoothly?
3   According to Richard Schoenberg, what is the biggest factor that can affect the success of a cross-border merger?
4   Managers of which nationality are particularly good at managing merger integration?

B   **Understanding details**

Read the article again and answer these questions.

1   What business is Air Liquide in?
2   What were the problems in the newly merged company, Air Liquide Deutschland?
3   What were the main challenges for Air Liquide Deutschland after the merger?
4   What were some of the 'emotional viruses' that threatened the success of the merger?
5   What use was made of the 12 'emotional viruses'?
6   What was the cultural awareness training project called?
7   How long did the training project last?
8   Are differences in national culture more important than differences in corporate cultures in mergers, according to the article?
9   What did Richard Schoenberg discover in the study he carried out?
10 What are Dutch managers good at during mergers, and why?

Why a successful merger is all in the mind

by Alison Maitland

A When Air Liquide, the French industrial gases group, acquired two-thirds of its German rival Messer Griesheim, the newly combined business was a breeding ground for cross-cultural misunderstanding and resentment.

B Just beneath the surface, conflicting work styles, national stereotypes and insecurity about the future threatened to undermine the new company, Air Liquide Deutschland, formed from the German operations of Air Liquide and Messer Griesheim.

C The management team decided to take swift action to expose problems and address them head-on. With the help of a specialist consulting firm, it interviewed employees and identified 12 'emotional viruses' that could weaken the merger.

D 'The main challenge was how to get people working together and retain customers so that we didn't lose business,' says Markus Sieverding, Air Liquide Deutschland's Chief Executive.

E Mr Sieverding's challenge will be familiar to senior executives from many other companies. Among the 'viruses' discovered were a strong belief by both sides in their own superiority, a fear of job losses at Messer, and anxiety at Air Liquide that its flexible management style would be deadened by German 'rationality'.

F Management appointed 35 employees across the merged business to raise awareness of the 'viruses', spot outbreaks and prevent them spreading. The list was used as a way of discussing concerns and anxieties at workshops where hundreds of employees were asked to help define a new way of working together.

G The 'mental merger' project ran parallel to the integration of business processes such as finance, administration, IT and logistics, says Mr Sieverding. 'It was really useful for the first three to six months to make it clear that these kinds of issues were being tackled and that we were not concerned only with the P&L and balance sheet.'

H Research into past cross-border deals suggests that about half of all mergers fail to meet their objectives, with culture clashes frequently to blame. Nationality can play a big part at the start. Differences in corporate culture may, however, play a more significant role in disrupting post-merger performance.

I Indeed, the evidence on the impact of nationality is mixed. Some studies have found that the bigger the national differences in cross-border mergers, the worse their performance. Others have found the opposite. 'It is a controversial area of research,' says Richard Schoenberg, Senior Lecturer in Strategic Management at Cranfield University School of Management in the UK. 'The effect of national culture may be slightly less than we believe because there are positive as well as negative aspects, and they may neutralise each other.'

J Schoenberg has examined differences in management style in 129 UK acquisitions of continental European companies in the 1990s. The only significant factor affecting performance was companies' attitude to risk: the bigger the difference between the bidder and target in their approach to risk, the less likely it was that the acquisition met its goals.

K Differences in attitude to risk probably indicate wider differences that may prevent a successful deal. Companies do not spend enough time on these issues before making acquisitions, says Mr Schoenberg. 'I strongly believe they should do much more organisational – as well as financial – due diligence.'

L Another consultant on mergers, Ulf Tworeck of Mercer Delta in Germany, believes the Dutch are particularly good at building bridges between merging companies. 'They're very strongly focused on the outcome … rather than taking political positions. I advise companies to look for Dutch executives for the integration phase, to bring warring factions together.'

FT

VOCABULARY

A **Understanding expressions**

Choose the best explanation for each phrase from the article.

1 '... a *breeding ground* for cross-cultural misunderstanding ...' (lines 4–6)

   a) new place
   b) fertile place

2 '... threatened to *undermine* the new company ...' (lines 9–10)

   a) make less strong and effective
   b) give support to

3 '... decided to *take swift action* to ...' (lines 14–15)

   a) take quick decisions
   b) do something very dramatic

4 '... expose problems and *address them head-on*.' (lines 15–16)

   a) define them clearly
   b) deal with them directly

5 '... would be *deadened* by German "rationality".' (lines 34–35)

   a) weakened
   b) killed

6 '... *spot outbreaks* ...' (lines 38–39)

   a) identify when problems appear
   b) describe new problems

7 '... these kinds of issues *were being tackled* ...' (lines 51–52)

   a) efforts were made to deal with the difficulties
   b) the problems were being identified

8 '... in *disrupting post-merger performance*.' (lines 61–62)

   a) preventing things from working well after the merger
   b) reducing income and profits after the merger

9 '... organisational – as well as financial – *due diligence*.' (lines 95–96)

   a) being careful before making an acquisition
   b) investigating fully before agreeing a deal

10 '... to bring *warring factions* together.' (line 106)

   a) departments which are very worried about the merger
   b) groups which disagree strongly with each other about aspects of the merger

B **Word partnerships**

Match these words to make noun–noun pairs from the article. Then match each noun–noun pair with a definition (i–v).

1 management	a) firm	i) when people of different nationalities do not get on well together
2 work	b) clashes	ii) a professional organisation which gives advice to companies
3 consulting	c) styles	iii) the way a company is run by its managers
4 management	d) team	iv) ways of working
5 culture	e) style	v) the group of executives who run a company

C Vocabulary development

Find words or phrases in the article which have the opposite meaning to these.

1 contentment, satisfaction (paragraph A)
2 compatible, similar (paragraph B)
3 strengthen (paragraph C)
4 lose (paragraph D)
5 inferiority (paragraph E)
6 rigid (paragraph E)
7 succeed (paragraph H)
8 occasionally (paragraph H)
9 widely accepted (paragraph I)

D Prepositions and verbs

When verbs follow prepositions, they are always in the -ing form.

Complete these sentences using the prepositions and verbs in the box.

Prepositions: at   before   from   in   of   of
Verbs: build   discuss   disrupt   make   spread   work

1 Employees were asked to help define a new way .... together.
2 Differences in corporate culture may play a significant role .... post-merger performance.
3 Companies do not spend enough time on these issues .... acquisitions.
4 The Dutch are particularly good .... bridges.
5 Management at Air Liquide Deutschland wanted to prevent the 'emotional viruses' ....
6 The list of emotional viruses was used as a way .... concerns and anxieties at workshops.

OVER TO YOU

1 The article mentions three 'emotional viruses' that could have weakened the merger: a strong belief by both sides in their own superiority, a fear of job losses at Messer, and anxiety at Air Liquide that its flexible management style would be deadened by German 'rationality'. What do you think some of the other 'emotional viruses' were?

2 According to Richard Schoenberg, differences in corporate culture, and in particular differences in companies' attitudes to risk, are more likely to disrupt post-merger performance than differences in national culture. What is your opinion?

3 The Dutch are described as being good managers to use to help make a merger successful. What cultural characteristics do you think make the Dutch particularly suitable for this role? Are managers from any other cultures likely to have similar qualities?

Rescuing a merger that's going wrong

This unit looks at what a new Chief Executive Officer (CEO) can do to rescue a merger which is going badly wrong.

BEFORE YOU READ

Discuss these questions.

1   Can you think of some international mergers which have not worked? What were the reasons?

2   What steps should the CEO of a newly merged company take to try to ensure that it will be successful, especially from a cultural point of view?

READING

A   **Understanding the main points**

1   Read the article on the opposite page and answer this question.

What was the main problem at Alcatel-Lucent before Ben Verwaayen was appointed as the new CEO?

2   **Match each of these pieces of advice to the person who gave it.**

1   A merger is an opportunity to change the culture of the new organisation right from the start.
2   It is important for the different cultures in a cross-border merger to learn how to work well together.
3   A newly merged company needs to have a common vision, which is shared by all senior managers and communicated to all employees.

B   **Understanding details**

Read the article again and say whether these statements are true (T), false (F) or there is not enough information given (N). Give your reasons.

1   Ben Verwaayen was previously Chief Executive of British Telecom.

2   Ben Verwaayen is Dutch.

3   When Alcatel and Lucent merged, the US culture became the dominant culture.

4   Before its acquisition by SAP, Business Objects had little experience of US business culture.

5   Integrating SAP and Business Objects managers into cross-border teams was a priority after that merger.

6   In all mergers, some managers will be unhappy with the new culture and will leave.

7   Changing the culture of the newly merged entity is not the most urgent priority. Improving income and profits are more important.

8   Immediately after a merger, a PR firm should be hired to manage all external communications.

9   It is important for all members of a merged company to share a common goal.

10   During the merger integration process, only positive news should be communicated. Problems and difficulties should be kept private.

Can new CEO end culture clash after merger?

by Alison Maitland

THE PROBLEM

A In late 2008, Ben Verwaayen, former Chief Executive of British Telecom, was named as the new CEO of Alcatel-Lucent, the telecommunications equipment group. For more than two years, the company had suffered from a mishandled integration following the 2006 merger of Alcatel and Lucent, which heightened cultural differences between its American and French arms.

B What actions can incoming executives take to resolve internal disagreements in a global business? Is improved performance the best cure for cross-border antipathy? Or should a new management team address cultural issues head-on?

THE ADVICE

C Cultural sensitivity is vital in running a global business. Before its acquisition by SAP, Business Objects was a French company with a strong US presence, in which managers worked to combine the best of French passion and creativity with American drive and teamwork. To achieve this, it is essential to encourage individuals to appreciate the other people in the mix.

D In the first six months after the acquisition, more than 35 per cent of senior managers transferred from SAP, while all of the original Business Objects corporate services people are now part of a global shared-services team. We also encourage cross-border, cross-functional teamwork on projects such as major product releases. In this way, team members come to depend on each other.

E My advice to business leaders is to embrace, not avoid, the strengths and differences of your global employees and turn them into a competitive advantage.
John Schwarz, Chief Executive of Business Objects, an SAP company

F The key is to describe a new culture that draws on the best of the past organisations but shows a more attractive way forward. A new CEO can do that, but must still find allies in the old factions. Together, they must personally demonstrate new ways of behaving, and it is best to be explicit about what these are. Inevitably, some executives will go: more often than not, cultural changes mean people change. What will not work is waiting for improved performance.

G The reason cultural problems matter is that they obstruct performance, and the need to improve performance is the best incentive to change culture. Besides, cultural change is easier when a company is challenged. This is the reason that such change had better start at the beginning of a turnaround.
Richard Rawlinson, Partner at Booz & Company

H Mergers are a delicate time in the history of any organisation, but good communication is the lifeblood of change. For Ben Verwaayen, pulling people together behind a common goal will be critical for success. His first task will be to ensure a collaborative leadership team. They must agree the corporate 'story' for the company, what it is and where it is going, and articulate this vision to staff. There will always be cultural differences across different parts of a global business. The problem that these have become public knowledge, potentially damaging Alcatel-Lucent's reputation.

I Once the senior team has agreed the direction of the company, it is vital to create a communications plan to keep each stakeholder in the business frequently and consistently informed about progress. This will help create a common culture, as well as making workers and the external audience aware of positive changes in the business.
Colette Hill, Chairman of CHA, a workplace communications consultancy

FT

VOCABULARY

A **Word search**

Find words or phrases in the article which fit these meanings.

1 something that is badly managed (paragraph A)

m........

2 increased, made worse (paragraph A)

h........

3 when people dislike each other (paragraph B)

a........

4 directly (paragraph B)

h........-o........

5 determination and energy to succeed (paragraph C)

d........

6 accept an idea openly and willingly (paragraph E)

e........

7 supporters (paragraph F)

a........

8 try to prevent something from happening by making it difficult (paragraph G)

o........

9 something that encourages you to start something new (paragraph G)

i........

10 when a situation changes from bad to good (paragraph G)

t........

11 the thing that keeps something strong, healthy and successful (paragraph H)

l........

12 when people work together to produce something (paragraph H)

c........

13 describe and explain something in clear language (paragraph H)

a........

14 be known by everyone (paragraph H)

b........ p........ k........

15 the opinion people have about how good or bad something is (paragraph H)

r........

16 a person or group that is involved in and can be affected by a particular organisation (paragraph I)

s........

B **Negative and positive phrases**

1   Find four phrases in 'The Problem' section which describe the negative aspects of cross-border mergers.

2   Find at least four positive expressions and recommendations in John Schwarz's advice on how to make cross-border mergers successful.

3   Find at least seven recommendations in Colette Hill's advice for helping cross-border mergers to work better.

C **Vocabulary development**

1   The word *cultural* is used five times in the article in combination with different nouns. Find the phrases by matching the nouns to these definitions.

1   things that people discuss and that need to be dealt with

2   when two or more groups do not think or behave in the same way

3   when things are done differently

4   being aware of the feelings of others

5   things that causes trouble or difficulty

2   What other phrases using *cultural* + noun can you think of?

D **Prepositions**

Complete these sentences using the prepositions in the box.

| for   from   into   on   on |

1   When a team works well, all the team members feel confident they can depend........each other.

2   Many cross-border mergers suffer........poor preparation concerning post-merger integration.

3   A successful merger will draw........the best aspects of both merger partners.

4   In an international merger, it is vital to plan in advance how different cultures can best work together rather than waiting........problems to arise.

5   Cultural differences can be a stimulus for creativity and new ways of thinking, so that cultural issues can be turned........a source of competitive advantage.

OVER TO YOU

1   Which of the three pieces of advice in the article do you like best? Why? Do you have any other advice to add?

2   Can you think of any examples where some of the recommendations in *The Advice* section have been used to help an international merger succeed?

3   A large international company is about to take part in a cross-border merger. They have asked you for advice to help the merger go as smoothly as possible from a cultural point of view. Discuss and decide what you would tell them. Consider the steps to be taken both before and after the merger.

This unit looks at some of the reasons for sending employees on international assignments and also some of the difficulties.

BEFORE YOU READ

Discuss these questions.

1 From a company's perspective, what are the benefits of sending employees on international assignments? And what are the disadvantages?

2 What are the benefits to the employee of living and working in a foreign country? And what are the challenges?

3 What countries or parts of the world could be considered as 'difficult' for employees from Western countries? Why?

READING

A Understanding the main points

Read the article on the opposite page and answer these questions.

1 What reasons are given in favour of sending employees on international assignments, especially to emerging markets in Asia?

2 What are some of the difficulties and disadvantages for companies of sending employees on international assignments?

B Understanding details

Read the article again and answer these questions.

1 How long will Claire Sandford spend in China?

2 What will be the benefit to her of having lived and worked in China?

3 What two international companies are mentioned in the article?

4 Why is it sometimes difficult to persuade some young professionals to work abroad?

5 What is HSBC's policy about international assignments?

6 Does HSBC insist that people go on an international assignment?

7 What can be the result if an HSBC employee does not want to go on an international assignment?

8 According to recent research, what are the costs of sending employees on international assignments?

9 According to research, what percentage of employees leave their company soon after returning from an international assignment?

10 Why do they leave?

11 What should companies do to try to prevent returning expatriates from leaving the company?

International assignments – challenges and opportunities

by Alicia Clegg

A Every week, Claire Sandford does battle with elementary Mandarin in between managing the requirements of clients in PwC's Beijing office.
5 By the time she and her husband return to London from her two-year secondment, the 34-year-old executive expects to have mastered the basics of the language and, through her expand-
10 ed professional circle, be firmly plugged into the fabric of the world's next economic superpower.

B Ms Sandford is just one member of a large army of career-minded pro-
15 fessionals criss-crossing the world to gain experience of emerging markets.

C Charles Macleod, Director of Resourcing at PwC – which has 1,200 employees from its global workforce
20 posted outside their home countries – explains why it pays to speed up the flow of skills from mature to developing economies. 'If you have someone in Europe who could produce twice as
25 much return in Asia, it makes sense to move them from markets in the northern hemisphere to parts of the world where activity is continuing to build.'

D Exposing promising employees to
30 emerging markets has become a strategic necessity. As Mr Macleod points out, tomorrow's multinationals will come from today's emerging markets. 'Wherever you trade, it is going to be
35 really important to have people who understand how business is done in Asia and the Middle East.'

E But persuading people to uproot themselves can be a battle. The big-
40 gest hurdle is the mismatch between the time when professionals are happiest to travel – when they are young and single – and the time when they have most to contribute as mobile
45 workers: after they have acquired skills, but also domestic responsibilities. So what happens when personal and professional considerations come into conflict?

F As one of the most geographically diversified banks, HSBC has a long-standing policy of sending its rising stars on international assignments. Sometimes a high-flyer may not want
55 to make a move abroad. In such situations, says Paul Ryder, HSBC's Head of Resourcing, the bank's policy is to respect the person's wishes. But the practical effect of missing out on
60 international experience is to slow and ultimately to cap an executive's progress through the business. 'As individuals, we all make choices and know that there are consequences
65 from those choices.'

G But one drawback of global mobility is its expense. Recent research by PwC and Cranfield School of Management showed staff on secondment
70 can cost three to four times their home-country salaries. They also need hours of administrative support. And many companies fail to recover their investment. Within a year of coming
75 home, 15 per cent of staff had left their organisations. In the worst cases, employers suffered attrition rates approaching 40 per cent.

H One explanation is that after prov-
80 ing themselves in another culture, returnees find coming home a big anticlimax. 'If you bring someone back to the desk they left three years before, the likelihood is that you have lost
85 them,' says Mr Gartside. 'To win the mobility battle, you have to demonstrate consistently that people who are willing to work abroad can jump stages in their careers.'

I In a global economy, businesses desperately need people who understand and feel at home in other cultures. Employers who mismanage the expectations of their returning
95 staff should not be surprised if they use the kudos of their international experience to explore avenues elsewhere.

FT

VOCABULARY

A Understanding expressions

Choose the best explanation for each phrase from the article.

1 '... *does battle with elementary Mandarin* ...' (lines 1–2)

   a) has arguments with her Chinese colleagues
   b) finds Mandarin a difficult language to learn

2 '... to *have mastered the basics* of the language ...' (lines 8–9)

   a) have a good basic knowledge
   b) know only a few basic expressions

3 '... *be firmly plugged into the fabric* of the world's next economic superpower.' (lines 10–12)

   a) have a good network of contacts
   b) understand the culture well

4 '... *criss-crossing the world* ...' (line 15)

   a) studying foreign cultures
   b) travelling frequently from one country to another

5 'But persuading people to *uproot themselves* ...' (lines 38–39)

   a) change their jobs
   b) move to another country

6 '... to *cap an executive's progress through the business.*' (lines 61–62)

   a) be the final stage in their career
   b) prevent their career advancing

7 '... *suffered attrition rates* approaching 40 per cent.' (lines 77–78)

   a) had large numbers of people who left the company
   b) had large numbers of people who complained about their assignment

8 '... returnees *find coming home a big anti-climax.*' (lines 81–82)

   a) suffer from culture shock
   b) are disappointed at the lack of new challenges

9 '... *the kudos* of their international experience ...' (lines 96–97)

   a) the experience they gained
   b) the benefit to their reputation and CV

B Word search

Find words or phrases in the article which fit these meanings.

1 when someone is sent somewhere else (often abroad) to do a different job for a limited period of time (paragraph A)

   s........

2 sent somewhere (usually abroad) to do a job there (paragraph C)

   p........

3 used to describe an employee who is likely to be successful in the future (paragraph D)

   p........

4 a problem or difficulty that you must deal with before you can do something else (paragraph E)

   h........

5   a combination of things that do not work well together (paragraph E)

m........

6   something that might be a problem or disadvantage (paragraph G)

d........

7   handle something badly (paragraph I)

m........

C   **Word partnerships**

Match the verbs (1–5) with the nouns (a–e).

1	to recover	a)	a return
2	to acquire	b)	experience
3	to produce	c)	at home
4	to feel	d)	skills
5	to gain	e)	their investment

D   **Sentence completion**

Use the word partnerships from Exercise C in the correct form to complete these sentences.

1   Consultancy companies always try to .... the best .... they can from their consultants' time.

2   People who live and work abroad have the chance to .... a lot of .... of different cultures.

3   Sending people to work abroad is very expensive, so it is important that companies .... by making good use of a returning employee's skills and experience.

4   People who have successfully lived and worked abroad for a number of years usually .... in foreign cultures.

5   Giving young employees different jobs, sometimes in different countries, enables them to .... that are essential for their future careers.

E   **Vocabulary development**

1   What other word is used in the text with the same meaning as *secondment*?

2   What is the verb form from the noun *secondment*? How do you pronounce it?

3   What other verb is used in the article with a similar meaning?

4   In paragraph F, two phrases are used to describe 'promising young employees'. What are they?

OVER TO YOU

1   Not all international assignments are successful. Sometimes the employee 'fails' and has to return home early, at considerable cost to the company. Define what 'to fail' on an international assignment means; then discuss and list as many reasons as you can think of why this might happen, and what some of the costs and consequences might be.

2   A company is having problems with returning expatriates. More than 30 per cent leave the company within a year of returning. Hold a management meeting to discuss the problem and to come up with some recommendations to reduce this high attrition rate.

Expatriate families

This unit looks at the pressures on expatriate families when they move from country to country.

BEFORE YOU READ

Discuss these questions.

1 Do you think the number of expatriates working abroad is increasing or decreasing? Why?
2 What are the main pressures on expatriate families caused by an international lifestyle?

READING

A ### Understanding the main points

Read the article on the opposite page and answer these questions.

1 What is special about the Lloyd-Hurwitz family?
2 Which of the two, Stuart or Susan, is the international executive?
3 How common is it for the spouse of an international executive to work in a foreign country?
4 What is one of the main causes of failure of overseas assignments?

B ### Understanding details

Read the article again and answer these questions.

1 What is the trend for overseas postings?
2 What is one of the main objectives of the spouses of international executives?
3 How many times have Stuart and Susan moved jobs, cities and countries?
4 What is Stuart's profession, and how successful has he been in finding work in foreign countries?
5 What percentage of spouses find a job when they move abroad with their partners?
6 What are some of the factors about living abroad that make spouses unhappy?
7 What did the GMAC survey show?

C ### Searching for figures

What do these percentages refer to?

1 2 per cent
2 60 per cent
3 20 per cent
4 89 per cent
5 62 per cent
6 28 per cent

No place like home

by Miranda Green

A When Stuart Lloyd-Hurwitz and his wife Susan sat down to watch the Beijing Olympics with their three children at home in London, the reality of their complex family allegiances became clear. Stuart is American, his wife is an Australian originally from the UK, and each child was born on a different continent and holds three passports. Stuart is one of a growing band of spouses who follow their partner's business career around the globe.

B In recent years, banks and corporations have been moving their top executives from city to city in a way previously seen only in the military or diplomatic service. Relocation companies estimate that up to 2 per cent of multinational corporate employees are working abroad at any one time, with the majority of companies expanding their overseas postings every year. And, unlike the diplomatic or military wives of the past, the modern spouses of these executives – the vast majority of whom are women – are attempting to build mobile careers of their own.

C Stuart has spent more than a decade inventing and then re-inventing his own working life every time his wife's high-flying career in property investment has led them to a new location. In the long run, the family intends to settle in Australia permanently, with one more move likely in the meantime. But up to this point, Susan's jobs have taken the couple, and then, as a daughter and two sons arrived, the whole family to four cities involving five moves.

D 'I've lost count, to be honest,' Stuart laughs, describing the journeys of his life so far, from his home town of New York, to his first job with Oracle in San Francisco, to business school at Insead near Paris, where he met Susan, then to Sydney, back to New York, back to San Francisco, then Sydney again, and now London. Each of the moves since he followed her to Sydney after their marriage has been dictated by his wife's career. The couple rejected only one assignment – to Hong Kong – and have been able to cope with lead-in times as short as two or three months every time.

E As a business consultant, Stuart has managed to either find employment or clients everywhere the family has moved, and his career has thrived. But not all so-called 'trailing spouses' are so fortunate: corporate employees who give up their own hard-won position to accompany a spouse find it increasingly difficult on each move to find a job at the same level; and many lack the drive and the business qualifications to make a success of their peripatetic life.

F A 2008 study by Nina Cole of Ryerson University in Toronto revealed that although 60 per cent of spouses are employed before expatriate assignments, only 20 per cent find employment while abroad.

G Lack of work, combined with culture shock, leaving friends and family, and the other stresses of transition for themselves and their children, can make trailing spouses miserable. And a growing body of research is emphasising that the needs of the relocating employee's family are often forgotten, with disastrous and expensive consequences for the individuals – and the employers – if the posting has to be cut short.

H The most recent global relocation trends survey from GMAC Global Relocation Services showed that family concerns accounted for 89 per cent of overseas assignment refusals and spouse career concerns for 62 per cent. Family was offered as the reason for 28 per cent of early returns, making it the most common cause.

FT

VOCABULARY

A Word search

Find words or phrases in the article which match these meanings.

1 loyalties (to a country) (paragraph A)

2 wives or husbands (paragraph A)

3 in a foreign country (paragraph B)

4 to start living in a place where you intend to stay for a long time (paragraph C)

5 relocations to other cities or countries (paragraph C)

6 times for preparation and planning (paragraph D)

7 developed very well, became very successful (paragraph E)

8 wives or husbands who accompany their partners on overseas assignments (paragraph E)

9 determination and energy (paragraph E)

10 moving from place to place (paragraph E)

11 the experience of trying to adjust to a new culture (paragraph G)

12 very unhappy (paragraph G)

13 very bad, often ending in complete failure (paragraph G)

14 worries (paragraph H)

B Word partnerships

Match these words to make word partnerships from the article associated with living and working abroad.

1	relocation	a)	shock
2	overseas	b)	spouse
3	home	c)	companies
4	trailing	d)	town
5	expatriate	e)	assignment
6	culture	f)	postings

C Sentence completion

Use words and phrases from Exercises A and B to complete these sentences.

1 Multinational companies are increasing the number of their ....

2 .... help expatriate families find a home in their new country and a school for their children.

3 Expatriate families sometimes change countries so often that they find it difficult to .... in one place for long.

4 Some expats travel so much that they never return to their ...., where they grew up.

5 Susan Lloyd-Hurwitz has had five .... so far in her career.

6 It is more often the .... rather than the international executive who feels .... in the new country.

7 Most people who move to another country suffer from .... at one time or another.

D Expressing figures and percentages

1 Which figures in the article correspond to these expressions?

1	almost a third	4	the vast majority
2	more than half	5	one in five
3	almost two-thirds	6	a very small percentage

2 Match the percentages (1–7) with the corresponding expressions (a–g).

1	80 per cent	a)	almost half
2	22 per cent	b)	two-thirds
3	9 per cent	c)	more than a quarter
4	47 per cent	d)	a third
5	27 per cent	e)	just over one-fifth
6	33 per cent	f)	four-fifths
7	66 per cent	g)	just under a tenth

E Interpreting opinions

Choose the best expression of the writer's attitude in each of these extracts from the article.

1 '... up to 2 per cent of multinational corporate employees are working abroad at any one time ... '
(lines 19–22)
   a) That's a high figure.
   b) That's a low figure.

2 'Stuart has spent more than a decade inventing and then re-inventing his own working life ... ' (lines 30–32)
   a) That's a short time.
   b) That's a long time.

3 '... with lead-in times as short as two or three months every time.' (lines 57–58)
   a) That's a short time, but acceptable.
   b) That's surprisingly short.

4 '... corporate employees who give up their own hard-won position to accompany a spouse ... ' (lines 64–66)
   a) They have to make a difficult career decision.
   b) They have to make a difficult financial decision.

5 '... only 20 per cent find employment while abroad. ' (lines 76–77)
   a) That's quite a low figure.
   b) That's quite a reasonable figure.

OVER TO YOU

1 According to the two surveys mentioned in the article, how well the family settles in to the new location is what can most affect the success of an expatriate assignment. Discuss and list the measures a company can take to try to ensure that things go well.

2 Giving expatriates and their family members intercultural training before going on an international assignment is one way to reduce the risk of failure. What topics would you include in an intercultural training session for an expatriate couple coming to your country?

3 Plan an intercultural briefing day for an expatriate family moving from the UK or the US to your country.

Bringing up children abroad

This unit looks at the findings of a survey by HSBC of what expatriates think about bringing up children in different countries.

Discuss these questions.

1 What factors would be important for a family with children moving to live and work in another country?
2 Which countries do you think would be the best postings for expatriate families with children? And which would be the least desirable?

READING

A Understanding the main points

Read the article on the opposite page and answer these questions.

1 What are the five main criteria used in the survey?
2 Which countries did well in the survey?
3 Which countries did badly in the survey?
4 Who is Boris Johnson, and what is one of his objectives?

B Understanding details

Read the article again and say whether these statements are true (T), false (F), or there is not enough information given (N). Identify the part of the article that gives this information.

1 The survey covered fewer than 20 countries.
2 Britain is the worst country for expatriates with children.
3 The survey covered six main categories.
4 Britain came last in four of the categories.
5 The survey responses were given by both adults and children.
6 Most expat children in Britain go to private schools.
7 The most important item in the survey was the diet of the children.
8 The best country for expatriates with children is Spain.
9 The main factor for parents' choice of a 'good country' to live in with children is cost.
10 Most children who spend time in Spain learn Spanish by the time they leave.
11 Children spending time in France are likely to do well at school.

Britain down expats' wish-list for children

by David Turner

A Britain is one of the worst places for expatriates to bring up their children, according to a survey of expats carried out by HSBC Bank International. 5 Comparing results from 14 countries, the study found that the UK does particularly badly when it comes to the cost of bringing them up. The only place that does worse in the overall 10 rankings for expat children is the United Arab Emirates.

B HSBC's survey measures each country's suitability for expat offspring using five factors that probably 15 owe more to an ambitious parent's priorities than their child's. These include how much time they spend outdoors, how much studying they do, and their opportunity to speak 20 a foreign language. Another of the criteria, the cost of raising children, reflects parent's financial concerns. The fifth – whether a child is likely to remain in the country when they 25 grow up – shows parents' perceptions of how much their child is enjoying life there.

C The UK ranks below average in four of the categories. The only exception 30 relates to the likelihood of children remaining in the country, in which it lies right in the middle. Britain's low rating in study time may surprise some analysts, since it has some of the 35 most famous private schools in the world – though their high fees may put them out of the reach of some expats.

D The UK also comes bottom of 40 a separate table for 'the healthiest expat children' because of their high tendency to eat junk food while watching television or playing computer games. This table, which was 45 topped by India, Australia, France and Spain, does not contribute to the overall rankings.

E Aaron le Cornu, Deputy Chief Executive Officer for HSBC Bank 50 International, said: 'We're not going for the views of what children want, as it's their parents who are dragging them around the world.' But he justified parental dominance over the 55 survey's questions and answers by saying: 'When people are making the decision to go and take up a life abroad, they are usually thinking about their career development, and 60 also "how will this impact on the development of my children?"'

F Parents worried about the bad influence of British habits on their offspring might consider relocating to Spain, 65 which tops the table as the best country for expat children. More than half of parents said bringing them up there was cheaper than in their own country. Children also have opportunities to 70 improve themselves by playing outdoors and learning the language.

G Coming just after Spain in the overall rankings were France, Germany and Canada, with France scoring high 75 on study time and Canada being the country which was considered the most attractive place to live long term. The survey was based on comparing habits and costs in the country the 80 expats were living in with their home country.

H London, the most common British destination for expats, is determined to boost its attractiveness. Business 85 leaders have been discussing London's 'livability' at meetings of a committee set up by Boris Johnson, the mayor, soon after he was elected, aimed at securing London's position 'as a top 90 capital city'.

FT

VOCABULARY

A Definitions

Match the words and expressions in italic in the extracts from the article (1–10) with their definitions (a–j).

1 '… one of the worst places for expatriates *to bring up* their children …' (lines 1–2)

2 '… in the *overall* rankings …' (lines 9–10)

3 'The UK *ranks* below average in four of the categories.' (lines 28–29)

4 '… the *likelihood* of children remaining in the country …' (lines 30–31)

5 '… high fees may *put them out of the reach* of some expats.' (lines 36–38)

6 '… *dragging* them around the world.' (lines 52–53)

7 '… parental *dominance* over the survey's questions …' (lines 54–55)

8 '… influence of British habits on their *offspring* …' (lines 62–63)

9 '… to *boost* its attractiveness.' (line 84)

10 '… aimed at *securing* London's position …' (lines 88–89)

a) considering or including everything

b) full control

c) to look after children until they are adults

d) to improve, increase the value

e) probability

f) making someone go where they do not want to go

g) has a particular position in a list that shows how good or important something is

h) children

i) place beyond the limit of someone's ability

j) getting something important, especially after a lot of effort

B Opposites

What are the opposites to the words in italic in these extracts from the article?

1 Britain is one of the *worst* places … (line 1)

2 … the UK does particularly *badly* … (lines 6–7)

3 The only place that does *worse* … (lines 8–9)

4 The UK ranks *below* average … (line 28)

5 Britain's *low* rating … (lines 32–33)

6 The UK also comes *bottom* of a separate table … (lines 39–40)

7 … which *tops* the table … (lines 65)

8 … the *best* country for expat children. (lines 65–66)

9 *More* than half of parents … (lines 66–67)

10 … *cheaper* than in their own country. (line 68)

11 Coming just *after* Spain … (line 72)

12 … the *most* attractive place … (lines 76–77)

C Sentence completion

Look at this chart showing the overall results of the HSBC survey. Based on the information in the chart, complete the sentences below, using words and phrases from Exercises A and B.

Overall results for offshore offspring

country	outdoor time	study time	cost to raise	languages spoken	remain in country	overall
Spain	2	4	1	1	5	1
France	3	2	5	3	4	2
Germany	6	6	11	3	3	3
Canada	4	7	/	14	1	4
Singapore	5	3	4	7	14	5
US	8	9	5	10	2	6
Australia	1	7	9	13	5	7
India	14	1	2	12	8	8
China	11	10	3	6	8	9
Belgium	13	12	8	2	11	10
Hong Kong	11	5	12	8	12	11
Netherlands	9	13	10	5	10	12
UK	9	11	14	10	7	13
UAE	7	14	13	9	12	14

Note: Each country received a score out of 14 for each section. The country with the lowest score is the best for each criterion. Scores are converted into a ranking, with 1 being the best and 14 the lowest. (Source: HSBC Bank International Expat Explorer Survey 08)

1 Spain is the .... country in which to .... children.

2 The Netherlands .... very low in the survey.

3 Hong Kong also did particularly .... badly in the survey.

4 India .... the table for the amount of time children spend studying.

5 Canada comes first in terms of the .... of children remaining in the country long term.

6 All the English-speaking countries score low in the .... results for the opportunity to learn a new language.

7 Britain has a lot of work to do to .... its image as an attractive country for expats with children.

OVER TO YOU

1 Do you agree with the HSBC survey's choice of criteria? Would you include any others?

2 If your country is included in the survey, do you agree with its ranking? And if your country is not included, how do you think it would rank based on the five criteria?

3 Look at the overall results of the survey. Do any of them surprise you? Why?

4 What country other than your own would you most like to live in and bring up children in?

5 Imagine you are members of a public-relations team which has been given the task of 'selling' your country as a destination for expatriates with children. Prepare a presentation to do this.

This unit considers the challenges of working in virtual teams.

BEFORE YOU READ

Discuss these questions.

1 How would you define a 'virtual team'? Have you ever been a member of one? If so, what was your experience like?

2 What are the benefits of virtual teams?

3 What are the difficulties of working in virtual teams?

4 What strategies can be used to ensure virtual teams work as well as possible?

READING

A Understanding the main points

Read the article on the opposite page and answer these questions.

1 How global is Jenny Goodbody's team?

2 What is one of the challenges she has with her team?

3 What does research on virtual teams generally show?

4 What is the most important thing needed for virtual teams to work effectively?

5 What is particularly important when a virtual team starts working together?

B Understanding details

Read the article again and answer these questions.

1 How many people are in Jenny Goodbody's team?

2 How often do they meet through a teleconference?

3 What is one way she has thought of to get round the problem of communicating across different time zones?

4 What would be the pros and cons of this?

5 How is a virtual team defined?

6 Why is trust hard to build in virtual teams?

7 What is the best way to build trust in virtual teams?

8 What does John Gill and David Birchall's code of practice for virtual teams include?

9 What is one important thing to do when an international team is first formed?

10 How should team co-ordinators handle communication with members of the team?

Virtual teams need to build trust

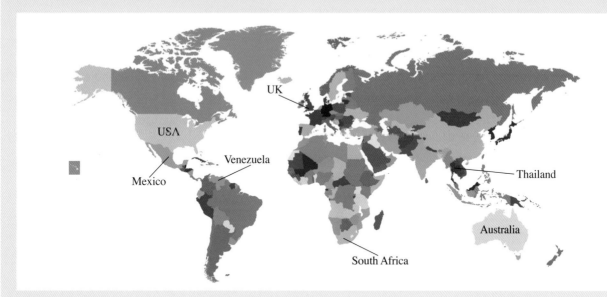

UK · USA · Venezuela · Mexico · Thailand · Australia · South Africa

by Alison Maitland

A Jenny Goodbody's team of six people is spread across six continents. Once a week, they meet through a teleconference, which means that she must be wide awake by 6.30 a.m. in New Jersey, while her colleague in Sydney, Australia, has to stay in work mode until well past 8.30 p.m.

B 'It's horrendously early in the morning for me and late in the evening for Australia,' says Ms Goodbody, Global Change Manager at Process Gas Solutions, a division of BOC, the industrial gases group which is now is now part of The Linde Group. 'I'm having a debate about whether we need to split into hemispheres and maybe do it once a month.'

C This would mean that at least two of the team would be less tired. On the other hand, some of them might feel more isolated if they had fewer opportunities to talk as a group.

D It is the kind of dilemma that faces any geographically dispersed team that has to communicate through e-mail, telephone calls or video conferences rather than face to face. While trust is crucial for every team to operate effectively, it is harder to build that trust among people who rarely, if ever, see each other.

E Ms Goodbody recently studied nine 'virtual teams' in her company for her MBA at Henley Management College in the UK. Only a third of them thought that they were successful in meeting their objectives – a finding that is in line with other research on virtual teams, she says.

F Part of the problem is that people working in a virtual team often assume that trust will come about automatically. 'The teams that were more successful put in an effort to try and build trust,' she says. 'They had short-term activities for people to work in pairs or threes, getting to know each other in smaller groups.'

G A face-to-face group meeting at the start is important. 'The teams that got together once could kick off that trust-building much more quickly. With the ones that didn't meet face to face, it was slower.'

H Virtual teams should agree a code of practice that sets out how to behave and communicate with each other, according to John Gill and David Birchall, two Henley academics, who have drawn up a framework for managers to build trust. The code should cover practical things, such as responding to e-mails within a fixed time. It should also cover psychological support, which could include sending encouraging messages and acknowledging the efforts of others.

I 'An important aspect of management behaviour, identified as supporting the development of trust, is consistency and its encouragement among other team members,' they add.

J Ms Goodbody found that the first stage, when the team is actually formed, is the most important in determining success. Team leaders can help to build relationships in different ways. 'They can try and get people to share some level of social information, for example about their country or their family.'

K As team co-ordinators, they also need to know how to summarise relevant information from the conversations that they have with individual members for the rest of the group. 'There's a fine line between making sure everybody is aware of what's going on and inundating people with e-mails they don't need,' she says.

FT

VOCABULARY

A Word search

Complete these sentences with words and phrases from the article.

1 If some members of a global team are not contacted very much, there is a danger they may feel i........ and cut off. (paragraph C)

2 A g........ d........ team is one where the team members are located in different countries. (paragraph D)

3 If something is extremely important, it is c......... (paragraph D)

4 Jenny Goodbody's study of the success rate of virtual teams was similar to, or i........ l........ w........, other research findings. (paragraph E)

5 The best way to build trust in international teams is to have f........ -t........ -f........ meetings at the start, so that people can get to know each other. (paragraph G)

6 A set of rules or guidelines on how virtual teams should communicate with each other is called a 'c........ o........ p........' by Gill and Birchall. (paragraph H)

7 'C.......' means not changing your mind or the message you give to different team members. (paragraph I)

8 One way for new team members to get to know each other is to exchange personal and s........ i......... (paragraph J)

9 A 'f........ l........' is where there is only a very small difference between two things. (paragraph K)

10 One aspect of good practice in international teams is to avoid i........ people with too many e-mails. (paragraph K)

B Word partnerships

Match the verbs (1–6) with the nouns (a–f) to form word partnerships from the article about working in teams.

1 to build
2 to summarise
3 to build
4 to determine
5 to meet
6 to form

a) success
b) objectives
c) information
d) a team
e) relationships
f) trust

C Opposites

Find words or phrases in the article which have opposite or contrasting meanings to these.

1 half asleep (paragraph A)
2 early in the morning (paragraph B)
3 frequently (paragraph D)
4 destroy (paragraph F)
5 long-term (paragraph F)
6 ignoring (paragraph H)
7 failure (paragraph J)

D Verbs and prepositions

Match the verbs (1–5) with the prepositions (a–e) to form phrasal verbs from the article.
Then match each phrasal verb with a definition (i–v).

1	to come	a)	up	i)	to start
2	to set	b)	off	ii)	to think of and write a list
3	to kick	c)	in	iii)	to happen, develop
4	to put	d)	about	iv)	to spend (time or effort doing something)
5	to draw	e)	out	v)	to explain or describe something in a clear and detailed way

E Sentence completion

Use the phrasal verbs from Exercise D to complete these sentences.

1 Before they start working, members of a virtual team should .... a team charter or set of guidelines on how to work together.

2 In the early stages when a team is formed, the team members need to .... time and effort to build trust.

3 All new teams should .... with a first meeting to get to know each other and build relationships.

4 A team charter should .... the behaviour and attitudes team members should have when working together.

5 A successful way of working as an international team does not .... easily. Everyone needs to work hard to build trust and follow a code of practice.

OVER TO YOU

1 You are members of a new global team meeting for the first time. In order to start building the team, do the following activity (based on an idea by Thiagi).
   a) Divide the team into four equal, small groups.
   b) Give each small group one of these questions:
      • What are you looking forward to about working in this team?
      • What are your doubts or fears about working in this team?
      • What kind of problems might arise in the team due to language, culture and distance?
      • What ideas can you think of to minimise problems that might be caused by language, culture and distance?
   c) Tell each group that they have 10 minutes to get all the other groups' input or responses to their question and also add their own ideas. (The best way to do this is by splitting up and interviewing the other groups.)
   d) Each group then reassembles and produces a summary of the input and responses they got to their question, including their own ideas.
   e) Each group in turn gives a short presentation of their key findings.

2 Based on the results of the previous activity, draw up a team charter: a set of guidelines for how best to work together and communicate with each other. Include both practical and psychological points.

A mixed-culture workforce

This unit looks at the effect of a mix of cultures at a European steel plant.

Discuss these questions.

1 What are the benefits and disadvantages of a mixed-culture workforce?
2 In your opinion, what are the relative strong points of German and French cultures, especially in the technical area?
3 What is a *melting pot*?

READING

A Understanding the main points

Read the article on the opposite page and answer these questions.

1 In which country is Dillinger Hütte located?
2 Why does it have a mix of German and French employees?
3 What does Paul Belche consider to be the strong points of German and French cultures in their approach to work?
4 Why does the writer choose the words of the article's title?

B Understanding details

Read the article again and answer these questions.

1 What is the connection between making mayonnaise and making steel?
2 What products does Dillinger Hütte produce?
3 How many people work at the Dillinger Hütte steel plant?
4 What is the proportion of German-speaking to French-speaking employees in the workforce?
5 Is Paul Belche German or French?
6 Which group – German speakers or French speakers – are better at plant safety, and why?
7 How is lunch organised in the company?
8 What services does Dillinger Hütte offer to its customers?
9 How difficult is it to make money out of making steel?
10 What does Paul Belche consider to be Dillinger Hütte's strength?
11 What other metaphor from cooking is used to describe the mix of cultures at Dillinger Hütte?

A melting pot for forging success

by Peter Marsh

A Paul Belche uses a culinary metaphor to explain how he tries to coax the best qualities from the mix of cultures at the steel plant he runs in western
5 Germany, close to the borders with France and Luxembourg.

B 'If you mix the yellow part of an egg with mustard and oil without being careful, you will produce something
10 unexciting. But if you pay correct attention to the details, you end up with the best mayonnaise,' he says.

C He is explaining his approach to managing Dillinger Hütte, a global
15 leader in specialist steels for applications such as oil pipelines. Mr Belche's tactics for getting the best out of his employees provide wider lessons for managers of diverse workforces.

D The company aims to take advantage of the different cultural characteristics of Saarland – the German state where it is based – that, over the centuries, has switched between French and
25 German sovereignty.

E Of the 5,500 employees in Dillinger, about 10 per cent have French as their main language, and the rest German. Mr Belche, a 56-year-old physicist, is
30 from Luxembourg.

F 'The Germans are strong when it comes to practical work. The French are good at theory, and we try to get the best of these two characteristics,' he says.

G Mr Belche poses a question: 'Who do you think would be better at plant safety – the German speakers or the French? You might think it would be the Germans. But actually it's the
40 French – they realise they are possibly behind in this field and so they work at it. Sometimes weakness can be a strength – as long as it's recognised.'

H His approach, he says, is to put teams
45 of people from the different cultures together and encourage them to learn from each other. The factory follows the French approach to dining, with a siren announcing the end of the
50 lunchtime break at 3 p.m., an hour later than is normal at other German steelworks. 'This is to give us time for a decent lunch,' says Mr Belche.

I When it comes to sales and tech-
55 nology, he says, the aim is to link the practical aspects of steelmaking and its applications, which he considers more German, and the theoretical, which he considers more French.

J The interest in developing both sides extends to inviting groups of customers to Dillinger, not just to tour the steelworks for hands-on demonstrations of the equipment, but also for scientific
65 seminars of up to 300 people, where the accent is on ideas.

K This mixing of the practical and theoretical must be linked to a single aim: making good products that will
70 do a better job of solving customers' problems, Mr Belche says.

L In the tough business of making money out of steelmaking, it helps if companies can offer something spe-
75 cial. In the effort to make this happen, the mix of cultures at Dillinger provides a soufflé of experiences, Mr Belche believes, that gives it a decent chance of success.

VOCABULARY

A **Word search**

Find words and phrases in the article which fit these meanings.

1 related to cooking (paragraph A)

2 to persuade, get something out of someone (paragraph A)

3 methods or plans for achieving something (paragraph C)

4 national rule over a country (paragraph D)

5 asks (a question) (paragraph G)

6 to connect (paragraph I)

7 to visit extensively (paragraph J)

8 practical, with real experience (paragraph J)

9 difficult (paragraph L)

B **Sentence completion**

Use words and phrases from Exercise A in the correct form to complete these sentences.

1 It's quite popular for some manufacturing companies to encourage visitors to .... the plant.

2 About every decade, the steel industry goes through .... times, when demand goes down.

3 You need to have good .... to get different cultures to work well together.

4 The best way to learn a practical skill is to have lots of ....-........ experience.

5 Managing a multicultural workforce well means trying to .... the best out of the mix of cultures.

6 Good international managers are successful at .... different cultures together.

7 Some parts of Europe have been under the .... of different countries during their history.

C **Word families**

1 Write the nouns for each of these verbs.

1	explain	7	announce
2	mix	8	develop
3	produce	9	demonstrate
4	manage	10	solve
5	recognise	11	provide
6	encourage	12	invite

2 Write the verbs for each of these nouns.

1	leader	4	strength
2	theory	5	sales
3	weakness	6	success

D **Prepositions**

Complete these sentences using the prepositions in the box.

at	at	between	from	of	on	out of	out of	to	to	with	with

1 If you pay attention .... details, you will get a good result.

2 The management skill is to mix one cultural group .... another.

3 The French are generally better .... theory.

4 Mr Belche wants to take advantage .... the diversity of the workforce.

5 It's important for the two cultures to learn .... each other.

6 By working .... something, you can become better.

7 If you invest the time and effort, you will end up .... something good.

8 When it comes .... practical work, the Germans are stronger.

9 In the seminars held at Dillinger Hütte , the accent is .... ideas.

10 Paul Belche wants to get the best .... his mixed-culture workforce.

11 Over the centuries, Saarland has switched .... German and French sovereignty.

12 Making money .... steelmaking is a tough job.

OVER TO YOU

1 When we make a generalisation about another group of people, it is often called 'stereotyping'.
Do you agree or disagree with the following statements about stereotypes? Give your reasons.

- National stereotypes are dangerous because they may create prejudice.
- Stereotypes contain a certain amount of truth and are therefore useful.
- There is no such thing as national character, and therefore the idea of national stereotypes is completely wrong.
- The reason stereotypes exist is because people are afraid of diversity and what is unknown. They prefer to hold on to simple classifications, which maintain an old, familiar and established order.
- Stereotypes are simply harmless sorts of jokes we tell about other nationalities or groups of people.

2 You may be familiar with this joke about heaven and hell in Europe, based on stereotypes of various nationalities. Can you complete the two descriptions with the list of professions in the box?

cooks	engineers	lovers	organisers	police

Heaven is a place where the ....[1] are British, the ....[2] are French, the ....[3] are German, the ....[4] are Swiss and the ....[5] are Italian.

Hell is where the ....[6] are British, the ....[7] are French, the ....[8] are German, the ....[9] are Swiss and the ....[10] are Italian.

3 What do you think of the two descriptions in the previous task? What stereotypes do they use? Do you find the descriptions amusing, or do you feel they are in poor taste?

Working in international project groups

This unit looks at the challenges of collaborating on projects with partners from many different countries.

BEFORE YOU READ

Discuss these questions.

1 If you have been involved in an international team or project group, how well did it work? What aspects worked well? What worked less well? What would you do differently next time?

2 What do you think are the most important things needed for project partners from diverse national and organisational cultures to be able to collaborate successfully? What might prevent successful collaboration?

READING

A Understanding the main points

Read the article on the opposite page and answer these questions.

1 Which of these statements best summarises the key message of the article?
   a) International project groups should not have more than nine partners.
   b) In large-scale international project groups, quick decision-making is vital.
   c) All parties in an international project team need to have a shared vision and goal.

2 According to the article, what three things are important for an international project group's success?

B Understanding details

Read the article again and say whether these statements are true (T), false (F) or there is not enough information given (N). Identify the part of the article that gives this information.

1 Markys Cain is a member of a global project group.
2 The MIND group that Markys Cain is a member of is collaborating on research projects.
3 Most of the MIND project group members come from universities.
4 All the partners in the MIND project share the same vision and goal.
5 All the partners also know exactly what their role in the project is.
6 In project groups with a lot of partners, decision-making can be very slow.
7 Decisions in the MIND group are taken at face-to-face meetings.
8 Most of the work in the MIND group is done through teleconferencing and videoconferencing.
9 Project teams work best if the partners share a common culture.

Making cultural diversity work

by Kim Thomas

A To be effective, modern organisations need to collaborate, whether through joint ventures, outsourcing relationships, or single projects for a
5 shared customer.

B Most organisations will have a number of partners, who may come from different sectors or countries. Each member of the group will often have
10 significantly different structures and processes. So what can go wrong, and what can companies do to make the process of collaboration as harmonious as possible?

C A prerequisite of success is a shared vision, says Markys Cain, Principal Research Scientist at the National Physical Laboratory (NPL). Mr Cain is an executive board member of the
20 EU's MIND Network of Excellence, a multi-disciplinary research collaboration between academic research organisations and companies from the UK, France, Germany, Switzerland,
25 Italy, Latvia, Spain, Denmark and Slovenia.

D A collaboration that involves parties from nine countries is inevitably going to have particular challenges
30 – especially when the cultural mix includes both universities and businesses, which have very different organisational cultures. The fact that the partnership is progressing well

35 and is on target to achieve its aims is partly because all partners are aiming at the same goal. 'If you spend the time working out what that vision is, and what you want to achieve, and you
40 get that right from as early as possible, you have a much greater chance of succeeding,' explains Mr Cain.

E Moreover, each organisation in the collaboration needs to recognise its
45 own niche or unique selling point. 'If everyone knows their position within a collaboration,' he adds, 'it makes it much easier to discuss things.'

F With such a large-scale venture,
50 there is a danger that it will collapse under the weight of different opinions. 'Decision-making in a large collaborative project can be difficult,' says Mr Cain. 'If you are so democratic that you
55 are taking referendums all the time, things take a very long time to change. Being decisive is extremely important.'

G The partnership has dealt with this by devising and implementing
60 particular mechanisms. Face-to-face meetings take place quarterly – or once a month during important phases of a project – and are reserved for taking decisions. Outside of those meetings,
65 smaller teams work on individual projects, and discussions take place through collaboration tools such as teleconferencing and videoconferencing, virtual workshops and shared
70 document areas on the web. Together, these speed up the processes and decision-making, says Mr Cain.

H In an ideal collaboration, each partner will play to its strengths. It is
75 not necessary for two organisations to have identical approaches or identical cultures: indeed, if they did, it would limit the opportunity for each to benefit from the other's expertise. The trick is
80 to find a way of working that benefits both parties. As one international manager puts it, the keys to a successful project are 'mutual trust, a shared goal and a fair proportion of the profits'.

FT

VOCABULARY

A Understanding expressions

Choose the best explanation for each phrase from the article.

1 'A *prerequisite* of success ...' (line 15)

   a) assurance
   b) requirement

2 '... is *inevitably* going to have particular challenges ...' (lines 28–29)

   a) unavoidably, definitely
   b) probably

3 '... *is on target* to achieve its aims ...' (line 35)

   a) is confident that it will
   b) has fixed a clear target

4 '... to recognise its own *niche or unique selling point*.' (lines 44–45)

   a) ability to sell
   b) special skills and strengths

5 '... by *devising and implementing* particular mechanisms.' (lines 59–60)

   a) organising and planning
   b) creating and using

6 '... each partner will *play to its strengths*.' (lines 73–74)

   a) concentrate on what it is good at
   b) try to improve

7 'The *trick* is to find a way of working ...' (lines 79–80)

   a) magical solution
   b) clever way of doing something

8 '... a *fair proportion* of the profits.' (line 84)

   a) reasonable part
   b) large part

B Prepositions and verbs

Complete these sentences by using a preposition and the correct form of the verb in brackets.

1 If all the partners of a project group share the same vision and goals, they will have a much better chance .... (succeed).

2 The company ensures good decision-making .... (organise) face-to-face meetings whenever a decision needs to be taken.

3 Other collaboration tools such as teleconferencing and videoconferencing should be reserved .... (exchange and share) information.

4 Most international project groups have different national and organisational cultures, so it is important to agree on a way .... (work) that suits everyone.

C **Word partnerships**

Match these words to make word partnerships from the article. Then match each
word partnership with a definition (i–vi).

1 joint   a) tools
2 cultural   b) venture
3 board   c) trust
4 organisational   d) mix
5 collaboration   e) member
6 mutual   f) cultures

i) a person sitting on the executive committee of a company
ii) when two or more people or organisations have confidence in each other
iii) when two organisations work closely together for a particular project
iv) devices or systems for communicating and sharing information more effectively at a distance
v) the combination of people or organisations from different cultures
vi) the values and way of working of individual companies or organisations

D **Opposites**

Find words and phrases in the article which are the opposites of these.

1 acrimonious (paragraph B)
2 possibly (paragraph D)
3 failing (paragraph D)
4 small-scale (paragraph F)
5 slow down (paragraph G)
6 weaknesses (paragraph H)
7 completely different (paragraph H)
8 expand, broaden (paragraph H)

OVER TO YOU

1 Markys Cain says that there are three requirements for successful collaboration in large project groups:
- Each partner should share the same aims and vision.
- Each partner must know what special skills or expertise it brings to the collaboration.
- There should be clear mechanisms and tools for decision-making, sharing information, etc.

Do you agree with him? Are there any other points you would add?

2 A new member has just joined the MIND project team. Use the ideas in the article to write or present a
set of guidelines about how the team works (a code of practice), to help the new member – include things
such as how decisions are taken, when and why teleconferences and videoconferences are used, etc.

This unit looks at an international graduate training programme run by Infosys.

Discuss these questions.

1 What do you know about Infosys? Which country is it from?

2 What do you understand by the term 'international graduate training programme'? What would the benefits be?

3 If you had the opportunity at the start of your career to work abroad for a foreign company, would you do it? What would expect to get out of it?

A **Understanding the main points**

Read the article on the opposite page and answer these questions.

1 Where does the Infosys international graduate training programme take place?

2 Why is Infosys running the programme?

3 What will the trainees learn on the programme?

B **Understanding details**

Read the article again and say whether these statements are true (T), false (F) or there is not enough information given (N).

1 Both the British and Indians are happy to multitask.

2 Infosys has never run a graduate training programme before.

3 The Infosys international graduate training programme lasts six months.

4 Infosys is a computer manufacturer.

5 Most of the trainees on the programme are from the UK.

6 Marco Cullen's major objective is to learn more about Indian culture.

7 Graduate training programmes in UK companies do not generally have an intercultural dimension.

8 Rick Mellor has discovered that global communications between different parts of Infosys are poor.

9 Infosys is running the programme to ensure it has a globally minded workforce.

10 Infosys is the only Indian IT company which runs an international graduate training programme.

An international outlook: Infosys Trainee Scheme

by Kate Hilpern

A 'If you visit a workplace in the UK, you'll generally find people approaching their daily tasks individually. If you visit a workplace in India, on the other hand, you'll find people are much more happy to multitask,' says Marco Cullen, who recently graduated from King's College London with a degree in electronic engineering and systems. 'You only have to look at their roads to see how comfortable they are with a lot of things going on at once!'

B Cullen only knows this because he was recently accepted onto Infosys's brand-new graduate training programme, which involves engineering graduates from around the world spending six months in India. Like a growing number of global companies, the provider of IT business solutions is investing heavily in ensuring that their graduates are able to work comfortably as part of an international, diverse workforce.

C The 25 graduates from the UK that have been selected onto this particular training programme recently arrived in Mysore, India, to join trainees from the United States, Japan, Australia, China and Mauritius. The idea is that they will all receive the same standard of high-quality technical training, while at the same time learning about the countries and communities around the world that they will ultimately operate in. 'It's already clear that this is going to be a big learning experience for us, both professionally and personally,' says Cullen.

D Cullen applied quite simply because the IT sector, like many others, is increasingly spreading its wings. 'You've got China and India, which have one billion people each, coming into the global economy. So the opportunity to experience different markets and work intimately with different cultures was too good to miss. I hope to end up with both the social and technical skills to equip me to work in a market that crosses national borders,' he says.

E But while more and more employers are jumping on the bandwagon, Cullen says all too many are getting left behind. 'If you look at a lot of the training schemes in UK companies, they might rotate you around various departments, but you rarely get to immerse yourself in the other cultures that you'll later be working with. Obviously that puts you at a disadvantage.'

F Rick Mellor, who has just graduated from the University of Bath with a degree in computer information systems and is also on Infosys's training scheme, agrees. 'While I was at university, I did a work placement at another global company and found the major issue it had was that the different global locations weren't that well connected. Communications between them were really quite poor.'

G BG Srinivas, Senior Vice-President of Infosys, says there are clear business benefits to training graduates overseas with peers from all over the world. 'A workforce that truly represent Infosys's global footprint and are able to work together in harmony are more likely to give the end user what they really need. That in turn helps us stand out,' he says.

H Even if graduates don't go abroad on every project they are involved in at Infosys, the chances are they'll be working as part of global teams, he says. 'This sector operates in a very diverse environment and if you put fresh graduates onto these large global projects without the kind of training we are offering them, the learning curve will be much slower,' he explains.

from The Independent

VOCABULARY

A Word search

1 Find words and phrases in the article which fit these meanings.

   1 totally new (paragraph B)

   2 very different from each other (paragraph B)

   3 expanding into new areas (paragraph D)

   4 to prepare someone to do something by giving them the necessary skills (paragraph D)

   5 starting to do something because a lot of other people are doing it (paragraph E)

   6 move someone from job to job to gain experience (paragraph E)

   7 to completely involve yourself in something (paragraph E)

   8 people who are the same age as you or have a similar job or position (paragraph G)

   9 be clearly better than others (paragraph G)

  10 people who have just left university (paragraph H)

  11 the time and difficulty involved in learning something new (paragraph H)

2 Find words or phrases in the article which all begin with the same four letters and have these meanings.

   1 an office or factory where people work

   2 the employees of a company

   3 when a student spends a short time as an intern at a company

3 Find six word partnerships starting with *global* in the article. Match them to these definitions.

   1 the different countries around the world in which a company operates

   2 companies operating in most parts of the world

   3 people from the same company working closely together but based in different countries

   4 the worldwide system by which goods and services are produced and used

   5 the degree to which a company operates in different countries around the world

   6 important pieces of work that are planned and organised over a defined period of time in different parts of the world

4 Infosys runs a graduate training programme. What other word is also used in the article instead of *programme*?

B Prepositions

Complete these sentences using the prepositions in the box.

around at in in on

1 Twenty-five graduates from the UK have been accepted .... the Infosys training programme.

2 In most graduate training schemes, the trainees are rotated .... different departments.

3 Because many UK graduate training programmes do not have an international component, the trainees are put .... a disadvantage for working with other cultures in the future.

4 Infosys is investing a lot .... ensuring that its future employees will be able to work effectively with people from other cultures.

5 Infosys wants to be sure that its internationally diverse workforce will be able to work together .... harmony.

C Vocabulary development

1 Think of words or phrases beginning with the same four letters as those in Exercise A2 which have these meanings.

1 spending time in a company to learn about the world of work

w........e........

2 a place in which tools are used to make or repair things; or a short training course to improve your skills

w........s........

3 the amount of work that a person has to do

w........l........

4 a document that enables you to work in a foreign country

w........p........

5 the part of an office where you work, including your desk, computer, etc.

w........s........

6 someone who does physical work, such as building

w........m........

7 a piece of paper with exercises on it that helps you to learn something

w........s........

8 someone who spends most of their time working

w........a........

2 Think of other word partnerships starting with *global* which match these definitions.

1 where trade can be carried out worldwide
2 the total amount of goods or services that people or companies buy or want to buy worldwide
3 a situation in which companies worldwide are trying to be more successful than others
4 the idea that the world can be considered as one unit for business and communication purposes
5 a general increase of world temperatures
6 a product that is known and sold all over the world

OVER TO YOU

Infosys has recently started a campaign, called 'Global Talent Programme', to recruit graduates onto its international graduate training programme. Use these notes to write an entry for the careers page of the Infosys website to attract international graduates to apply for the Infosys programme.

- Infosys – a global leader in next-generation IT services and consulting
- 91,000 employees from over 70 nationalities in more than 25 countries
- Global Talent Programme – different from other training schemes in the IT industry
- Gives international experience within an emerging market economy
- Six months on an intensive training course near Bangalore
- Future career options in business development and relationship management, project management, and technical specialist areas
- Qualities and skills needed – analytical, love solving problems, open-minded, keen to experience new cultures and new concepts

This unit looks at a professional development programme that aims to improve the quality and skills of international leaders.

BEFORE YOU READ

Discuss these questions.

1 What skills and qualities should a good international manager or leader have?
2 What should an international professional development programme for leaders and senior executives consist of?
3 What are some of the challenges future international leaders will face?

READING

A Understanding the main points

Read the article on the opposite page and answer these questions.

1 What kind of things did David Weekley learn from his visit to China?
2 What is the broad aim of international programmes such as Leaders' Quest, which are designed for future global leaders ?

B Understanding details

Read the article again and answer these questions.

1 What is David Weekley's job, and where is he from?
2 Who organised David Weekley's trip to China, and why?
3 What was the impact of the trip on him?
4 What was the background of David Weekley's companions on his visit to China?
5 Where in China did the group go, and how long did they stay?
6 What can leaders learn from visits to emerging countries such as China?
7 What impressed David Weekley about China?
8 What aspect of China worried him?
9 What did he do when he returned from China?
10 What was the result of Ashridge Business School's research?

Travel broadens executive minds

by Alison Maitland

A David Weekley, Chairman of a US house-building company, used to think he was well travelled and knowledgeable about the world. Then he went to
5 China on an international programme designed for senior leaders.

B 'I found I had a pretty warped view of the world,' says the 55-year-old Texan entrepreneur. 'When you reach
10 a position of success, you're often surrounded by folks who tell you you're right about things and you often enjoy an elevated position of power and influence. This took me down
15 a few notches.'

C The visit was arranged by Leaders' Quest, a non-profit organisation that aims to improve the quality of leadership around the world by bridging
20 divides between sectors and cultures. Mr Weekley's fellow participants included leaders from government, charities, business and academia in six countries. They visited Shanghai and
25 then Chengdu in Sichuan province.

D Interest in innovative programmes for individuals and senior teams is growing, says Leaders' Quest. In spite of the economic crisis, the organisation
30 says it is receiving more requests for information than ever before.

E According to research led by Ashridge Business School for a project called Global Leaders of Tomorrow, 76 per
35 cent of business leaders polled in 2008 said senior executives needed more skills and knowledge to respond to trends such as climate change and emerging market challenges. But less
40 than 8 per cent believed such skills were being developed effectively.

F Established and aspiring leaders alike can learn much from programmes designed to benefit them and the
45 emerging markets they visit, from greater self-knowledge to broader awareness of other cultural perspectives and understanding of global interdependence.

G For Mr Weekley, the intensive seven days of discussions and field visits, which covered business, education, science, culture, human rights and the environment, was an eye-opener. The
55 speed of China's development left him feeling that the US was, at least in some respects, being left behind.

H He was impressed by the motivation of entrepreneurs and schoolchildren, but
60 also troubled that China's one-child policy meant each child had the undivided attention of two parents and four grandparents. 'It's very hard to be "other-centred" if you're the centre of
65 attention for six adults,' he says.

I Equally enlightening were his companions on the quest. 'I got to see my own lack of knowledge as contrasted with their broader knowledge in a
70 wealth of areas, so it demonstrated how backward I was in terms of my worldly understanding,' he says. 'Being American, sometimes we think the world revolves around us.'

J On his return home, he decided to act. He hosted events for nearly 100 Texan businesspeople to learn about Leaders' Quest. So far, six have been on visits to Africa, Brazil, China and
80 Russia. He also went on another quest – typically costing £9,000 excluding flights, though bursaries are available – to Mumbai and Bangalore. The contacts he made led him to outsource
85 some architectural business to India. He donates funds to both countries and is involved in a micro-finance project in India.

K Did the experience change him as
90 a leader? 'It humbled me,' he says. 'It made me more open-minded. It made me not jump to conclusions or take everything I read in the media at face value.'

L This greater cross-cultural sensitivity is a key reason why Mr Weekley believes investment in international leadership development remains valuable, in spite of the economic crisis.
100 'Those that choose to go, and get to go, will have a much higher likelihood of future success in our changing world,' he says.

FT

VOCABULARY

A Word search

1 Find five positive words or expressions which David Weekley uses to describe himself, either before or after his visit to China, and match them to these definitions.

   1 having visited a lot of countries
   2 knowing a lot about things in the world
   3 interested in hearing about new ideas and ways of doing things
   4 think about things before making judgements
   5 doubtful about the truth of what is written in newspapers

2 Find four negative things that David Weekley says about himself or Americans in general and match them to these definitions.

   1 seeing the world through a very distorted lens
   2 how little he knew about many things
   3 having a very poor understanding of things in the world
   4 thinking they are the centre of everything

3 Find three reactions that David Weekley expressed after his visit to China and match them to these definitions.

   1 It made him a bit less confident about himself.
   2 an event that made him realise some surprising facts
   3 It made him realise that he was not as good or important as he thought he was.

B Vocabulary development

The following are all qualities which international leaders should have. Rearrange the words to make phrases used in the article.

1 knowledge greater self .
2 perspectives broader other awareness cultural of
3 interdependence global of understanding
4 cross greater sensitivity cultural

C Prepositions

Complete these sentences using the prepositions in the box.

about about around between by for from in in in of of of to

1 There is a growing interest .... the programmes organised by Leaders' Quest.
2 David Weekley says that Americans sometimes think the world revolves .... them.
3 Before his visit to China, Mr Weekley had a pretty warped view .... the world.
4 One aim of the visits arranged by Leaders' Quest is to make senior people from different cultures more knowledgeable .... the world.
5 Another aim is to bridge divides .... different cultures.

6 The Leaders' Quest programmes are designed .... senior leaders.

7 According .... research carried out by Ashridge Business School, senior executives need more skills and knowledge to be effective in a global world.

8 Leaders can learn a lot .... programmes such as those organised .... Leaders' Quest.

9 Since his visits to China and India, David Weekley has become involved .... several projects in those countries.

10 He also organised events in his native Texas so that senior Texan businesspeople could learn .... Leaders' Quest.

11 Mr Weekley believes that investment .... international leadership development is extremely valuable.

12 He also believes that leaders who go on visits like he did will have a much higher likelihood ...... future success In a changing world.

13 Mr Weekley believes that investment in international leadership development remains valuable, in spite .... the economic crisis.

OVER TO YOU

1 Based on the article and this extract from the Leaders' Quest website (www.leadersquest.org), what do you think of the aims of the organisation?

What is a Quest?

- It is an intensive programme of meetings, field visits, discussions and workshops held in stimulating and challenging parts of the world.
- It is about learning through engaging with diverse leaders – political, business and community – and ranges from meeting celebrated, well-known leaders to unsung heroes who are doing important but often unrecognised work.
- It provides the broadest exposure to each country by offering a diverse range of contrasting, 'on-the-ground' experiences – from visits to factories, retail stores and high-tech parks, to engaging with residents in slum communities and townships, or meeting with children and students in some of the world's leading schools and universities.
- It explores both the differences and common ground amongst leaders from diverse backgrounds, looking for what is inspiring and educational, and seeking out leaders who, in their own way, are striving to make the world a better place.
- It spans both the 'macro' issues of the region and the role it plays in the world, and 'micro' examples on the ground, exploring leading regional companies, organisations and communities.
- It includes regular group 'Reflection Time' through the course of the Quest so that participants may share key insights, questions and impressions, thereby refining their personal learning and development.

2 Would you like to go on a Quest? If so, present your arguments to your company or organisation to support your request.

Hiring university graduates from China

This unit looks at the growing trend for Western companies to hire Chinese university graduates.

BEFORE YOU READ

Discuss these questions.

1 How common do you think it is for Chinese university graduates to be hired by Western companies to work outside China?

2 Why should Western companies do this?

3 What do you think would be the main challenges for Western companies when hiring Chinese graduates?

4 What are some of the main cultural differences between Western countries and China?

READING

A Understanding the main points

Read the article on the opposite page and answer these questions.

1 Why should Western companies want to hire Chinese graduates to work outside China?

2 What are the benefits for a Chinese graduate in working for a global corporation?

3 What are the challenges for Chinese graduates when attending recruitment interviews with Western companies?

4 What is the main difference in relations between a boss and his/her subordinates in China and in the West?

B Understanding details

1 What are two disadvantages for Eric Lin about working in London rather than in China?

2 What has led to the trend of Chinese graduates working abroad?

3 How many graduates is PwC planning to recruit in China this year?

4 Where will PwC find the Chinese graduates to join their offices outside China?

5 What is one particular difficulty for Western companies when interviewing Chinese candidates?

6 How does Suwei Jiang get round this problem?

7 What helps Chinese people adapt to work and life in Western countries?

8 How would you describe Helen Zhi's personality?

9 Is her communication style typically Chinese? If it is different, how is it different?

China's new wave heads west

by Alicia Clegg

A Eric Lin, an associate lawyer seconded from Allen & Overy's China practice, is enjoying life in London. But he worries that while he is away, his colleagues and clients in Shanghai are making ground-breaking deals without him. 'Gaining experience and contacts abroad will ultimately help me,' he says. 'But maintaining my network in China is a big challenge.'

B The once unthinkable phenomenon of Chinese nationals such as Mr Lin joining foreign corporations has come about through China's assimilation into the world economy.

C China's emergence on the world stage has far-reaching consequences for Western-owned firms. In the past, multinationals hired Chinese graduates to staff their operations in China, says Charles Macleod, Global Resourcing Director at PwC. In the future, they will also increasingly need China specialists around the world to do business with Chinese companies that go abroad.

D 'We foresee a lot of opportunities to work with Chinese clients seeking to invest in other markets,' Mr Macleod says. This year, PwC is recruiting 1,700 Chinese nationals, who will train in its China practice. A smaller group, recruited from universities in English-speaking countries, will join its practices in Britain, Australia and the US. 'Our aim is to have a cohort of people who can support our clients wherever they do business.'

E For Chinese graduates, a spell with a global corporation confers kudos, access to other lifestyles and opportunities to pick up skills that are marketable in China and internationally transferable. But working in a foreign language and culture makes big demands of people, both personally and professionally.

F For employers seeking to recruit Chinese graduates, the top concern is to find the best people. Cultural complications make this trickier than it sounds. The first challenge when interviewing non-native speakers is distinguishing linguistic performance, which coaching can improve, from ability to think, which is harder to train and ultimately matters more.

G Suwei Jiang, a Director of PwC's China Business Centre in the UK, vividly recalls her own stumbling attempts to express herself succinctly before selection boards. Now, when she interviews for PwC's China office, she helps candidates give a good account of their abilities by using both English and Mandarin. If a candidate gives a poor response in English, she returns to the topic later in the interview in their own language. A better response second time around implies the applicant has difficulty expressing their ideas in a foreign language, not in thinking.

H Helen Zhi, a senior manager in KPMG's high-growth markets practice, says that, in her experience, Chinese people are perceptive observers. In an unfamiliar setting, they watch for cultural cues and adjust their behaviour to mirror that of their hosts.

I Yet misunderstandings still arise. As a young professional in China, Ms Zhi learned to control her natural talkativeness when attending meetings with her boss. When she came to Britain, naturally enough, she assumed the same rules applied. 'In China, my role was to observe and support my manager, not to speak. Here, even the most junior people are expected to give their views. But nobody told me that. It was something I had to work out for myself.'

FT

VOCABULARY

A **Word search**

Find words or phrases in the article which fit these meanings.

1 contracts or agreements in business (paragraph A)

    d........

2 provide the workers for an organisation (paragraph C)

    s........

3 predict (paragraph D)

    f........

4 group of people sharing a similar characteristic, usually age (paragraph D)

    c........

5 short period of time (paragraph E)

    s........

6 more difficult (paragraph F)

    t........

7 emphasising the most important part of something (paragraph F)

    u........

8 clearly and briefly, when speaking or writing (paragraph G)

    s........

9 place or time where something happens (paragraph H)

    s........

10 actions or events which help you decide what to do or understand what is happening (paragraph H)

    c........

11 match or copy the behaviour of another person (paragraph H)

    m........

12 find an answer or solution to something (paragraph I)

    w........ o........

B **Definitions**

Match these adjectives from the article (1–5) with their meanings (a–e).

1	ground-breaking	a)	hesitating and making mistakes when speaking
2	unthinkable	b)	good at noticing things
3	far-reaching	c)	involving important new discoveries or methods
4	stumbling	d)	very extensive
5	perceptive	e)	impossible to imagine or accept

C Sentence completion

Use the words and phrases from Exercise B to complete these sentences.

1 Twenty years ago, it would have been .... for Western companies to hire Chinese graduates outside China.

2 To be successful when working across cultures, it is important to be ...., to notice what people are thinking and feeling based on their words and actions.

3 If you are not a fluent speaker of a language, you are likely to give a very .... performance when presenting to an audience.

4 Most research scientists hope they will make a .... discovery one day.

5 Decisions taken now by Western companies about investment in markets such as India, China or Russia will have .... results in the years ahead.

D Vocabulary development

1 The verb *to hire* is used several times in the article. What other verb is used with a similar meaning?

2 What two words are used to describe a person who attends a job interview?

3 Complete the chart.

verb	noun	adjective
.... 1	emergence	 2
invest	 3	 4
recruit	 5	 6
interview	 7	 8
.... 9	response	 10
.... 11	observer	 12
adjust	 13	 14

OVER TO YOU

1 Imagine you are an intercultural consultant. What advice would you give to managers who will need to interview Chinese candidates for international jobs?

2 A Western company has recently hired some Chinese graduates to work with Western colleagues. What do you think would be some of the cross-cultural challenges that could arise when they work together? Some issues could be:
   • Different attitudes to hierarchy, seniority and status
   • Individualism vs. group orientation
   • Different learning and communication styles

Check Test 1 (Units 1–9)

A **Use words and phrases from Units 1–9 to complete these sentences.**

1 One of the most important aspects of culture are v........, the principles and beliefs that influence the behaviour and way of life of a particular group or community.

2 Cultures also have different b........, things which people in that culture consider to be true.

3 Another important aspect of culture is the way people think, in other words the a........ they have.

4 Differences between cultures can create b........, so that understanding and communication become difficult.

5 Some cultural differences are very visible, such as d........ (the clothes people wear).

6 The most visible difference between cultures is b........, such as styles of greeting, the use of names and ways of interacting in general.

7 Most Asian cultures prefer their managers to be d........, to show that they are in charge.

8 When we work with people from other cultures, we usually start off with e........ of how they will behave.

9 Research has shown that there are significant differences in personality t........ between business leaders from different countries.

10 Leaders in Asian countries put a lot of emphasis on maintaining group h........ and avoiding open disagreement.

11 People who are very direct in their communication style can come across as rather a........ and non-caring.

12 A major challenge between people from different cultures is to f........ o........ exactly what people mean.

13 Adapting behaviour when working across cultures is c........; unless you do this, you will not succeed.

14 The decision-making process in Japan is based on v........ consent – everyone must agree.

15 Another characteristic of Japanese working style is m........ planning, where everything is done very carefully.

16 When people work across cultures, some m........ and mistakes are inevitable.

17 Getting people to work in c........-b........ teams is a good way to promote greater cross-cultural understanding.

18 The better people understand each other's culture, the less likelihood there is of c........ c........ and other disagreements.

19 When companies use cultural differences in a positive way, they can gain a real c........ a........ over their competitors.

20 Mergers between companies in a similar business area can produce e........ of s........, thereby reducing costs.

B **Choose the best word or phrase to complete each of these sentences.**

1 When doing business in a foreign country, it is important not to offend.........
   a) local superstitions   **c)** national institutions
   b) local sensitivities   **d)** national behaviour

2 Reaching........ is an important aspect of Dutch and Swedish business culture. Everyone needs to be consulted before a decision is reached.
   a) decisions   **b)** argument   **c)** consensus   **d)** democracy

3 When two companies merge, it is important for the management to create a feeling of........, so employees feel positive about the merger.
   a) goodwill   **b)** friendliness   **c)** satisfaction   **d)** happiness

4 When entering a foreign market, it is important for companies to make .... to their core business model.

a) adaptations **b)** adjustments **c)** amendments **d)** refinements

5 Many companies in southern Europe have a .... structure, where all major decisions are taken at the top.

a) heavy **b)** formal **c)** family **d)** hierarchical

6 Geert Hofstede chose IBM for his famous study on the effect of culture on organisations because IBM had a very strong ....

a) corporate culture **b)** work ethic **c)** management style **d)** product range

7 Large companies in Japan need to show a strong sense of .... because of their important role in the community.

a) profitability **b)** customer loyalties **c)** social responsibility **d)** employee awareness

8 Trying to import a successful domestic business model into a foreign market without adapting it is a common .... for companies.

a) strategy **b)** goal **c)** approach **d)** pitfall

9 For a merger to be successful, it is important that the post-merger .... phase is handled well.

a) adaptation **b)** integration **c)** adjustment **d)** co-operation

10 An important personality trait for being successful across cultures is .... to new experiences.

a) readiness **b)** acceptance **c)** interest **d)** openness

11 When companies from two or more cultures come together, the leaders need to find a way of working together in a .... way.

a) communicative **b)** friendly **c)** collaborative **d)** decisive

12 The aim of some mergers is for one partner to gain knowledge and .... from the other.

a) income **b)** expertise **c)** profits **d)** turnover

13 If problems arise soon after a merger takes place, they need to be addressed ...., rather than left to grow and get worse.

a) head-on **b)** hands-on **c)** conscientiously **d)** sensibly

14 If cultural issues arise in a merger or joint venture, they need to be .... quickly, before they start to undermine the new company.

a) observed **b)** identified **c)** tackled **d)** described

15 A big challenge for Indian IT companies is how to persuade employees not to .... from job to job.

a) leave **b)** apply **c)** change **d)** hop

16 Foreign companies operating in China often have problems because of the .... nature of local regulations, which makes planning difficult.

a) unpredictable **b)** expensive **c)** different **d)** slow

17 In Japan, if a company does something wrong and upsets ...., its reputation can be damaged for many years.

a) the media **b)** its suppliers **c)** the tax authorities **d)** public opinion

18 The Schindler company is still trying to .... its image in Japan.

a) renovate **b)** resell **c)** rebuild **d)** renegotiate

19 Schindler's failure to apologise for the accident with one of its elevators was a big ...., which showed how little the company's top management understood about Japanese culture.

a) misunderstanding **b)** misjudgement **c)** insult **d)** mismanagement

20 Dell used an adapted version of its .... business model when it set up operations in China.

a) core **b)** central **c)** former **d)** new

Check Test 2 (Units 10–18)

A **Use words and phrases from Units 10–18 to complete these sentences.**

1 An e........ is someone who lives and works in country other than their own.

2 Some companies suffer high a........ r........, because employees returning from a job abroad then leave the company.

3 A lot of international companies have a policy of sending young high-flyers on an international a........ early in their career.

4 Many of these overseas p........ are to emerging countries, especially in Asia.

5 Global companies need employees who understand and f........ at h........ in other cultures.

6 When young professionals start a family, they are sometimes less willing to u........ themselves and move abroad.

7 T........ s........ often find it more difficult to adapt to a new culture than their working partner.

8 Most people who move abroad suffer from c........ s........ during the first year of their stay.

9 According to a survey carried out by HSBC, Britain is one of the worst countries for expatriates to b........ u........ children.

10 A v........ team is one that mainly communicates by phone and e-mail, and rarely meets face to face.

11 For a global team to work well, it is important to b........ t........ at the start of their work together.

12 Global teams should agree a c........ of p........, or a set of guidelines, that sets out how they should work together.

13 Some cultures react best to practical, h........-o........ demonstrations; others prefer a more theoretical approach.

14 If we generalise about a culture and its characteristics, we are in danger of creating s.........

15 Each company and organisation has its own distinctive o........ c........, which can sometimes be more of a barrier in international mergers than differences in national culture.

16 Indians are good at m........, unlike north Europeans, who generally prefer to do one thing at a time.

17 Global companies need to get the best from their international, d........ workforce.

18 One aim of intercultural training is to help people develop greater tolerance and a........ of other cultures.

19 A culturally sensitive person has a good understanding and acceptance of different cultural p........ or ways of looking at the world.

20 Another characteristic of a culturally sensitive person is to be o........-m........, ready to accept differences.

B **Choose the best word or phrase to complete each of these sentences.**

1 A........ abroad is essential for people who want an international career.

   a) practice **b)** work **c)** secondment **d)** visit

2 In overseas assignments, it is usually the spouse and family who find it difficult to .... in the new country.

   a) settle **b)** remain **c)** stay **d)** perform

3 Some people's careers really .... when working abroad, and they become very successful.

   a) increase **b)** perform **c)** accelerate **d)** thrive

4   Not every family adapts well to the .... lifestyle of an international executive.

   a) travelling   **b)** peripatetic   **c)** expensive   **d)** interesting

5   Adjusting to a new culture can be a steep .... for young professionals.

   a) learning curve   **b)** experience   **c)** lesson   **d)** milestone

6   The best way to understand a new culture is to .... yourself in it completely.

   a) bury   **b)** maintain   **c)** experience   **d)** immerse

7   Young graduates often try to get a(n) .... in a company abroad, so they can gain international experience.

   a) appointment   **b)** work permit   **c)** work placement   **d)** workload

8   A .... for success in international project groups is that the members need to have a shared vision.

   a) prerequisite   **b)** measure   **c)** sign   **d)** assumption

9   In a project group with members from many countries, being .... when taking decisions will help to keep things moving.

   a) creative   **b)** competitive   **c)** imaginative   **d)** decisive

10 When being interviewed for a job, being able to explain things .... , without using too many words, is an important skill.

   a) succinctly   **b)** interestingly   **c)** fluently   **d)** amusingly

11 When companies set up operations in a foreign country, they should .... the subsidiary branch with local people.

   a) recruit   **b)** hire   **c)** staff   **d)** organise

12 People who are successful when working with other cultures are usually very .... They can interpret what people mean by observing their actions carefully.

   a) communicative   **b)** perceptive   **c)** flexible   **d)** open-minded

13 If you watch how people from another culture behave, you can take your .... from them on how you should behave too.

   a) insights   **b)** example   **c)** cues   **d)** suggestions

14 Giving people intercultural training before they go on an international assignment reduces the need for them to .... things out for themselves.

   a) work   **b)** plan   **c)** make   **d)** take

15 The city of London is planning a campaign to .... its image in the eyes of expatriates with children.

   a) renew   **b)** revise   **c)** build   **d)** boost

16 Newly formed teams should always .... with a face-to-face meeting so that team members can get to know each other.

   a) kick off   **b)** move on   **c)** take off   **d)** build up

17 A successful international team is one in which the team members .... well with each other.

   a) negotiate   **b)** plan   **c)** organise   **d)** collaborate

18 Developing cultural .... is one of the main aims of intercultural training courses.

   a) perception   **b)** awareness   **c)** trust   **d)** experience

19 To succeed in its work, an international team needs to .... a good way of working together.

   a) propose   **b)** maintain   **c)** devise   **d)** allow

20 A good leader of an international team will be able to .... the different qualities and skills of the team members together.

   a) link   **b)** make   **c)** adjust   **d)** compare

Answer key

Reading

A 1 F (*Most companies, in fact, start dipping their toes into foreign waters long before they reach domestic saturation ...* (lines 6–8))

2 N (No best way is suggested. Setting up subsidiaries is only one way.)

3 F (*It had been known for years that working across cultures poses special problems ...* (lines 15–17))

4 T (*... Hofstede showed that a huge variety of beliefs and values were present in the workplace ...* (lines 25–27))

5 F (*Much more difficult to manage are the cultural differences that arise ...* (lines 62–63))

6 N (China is given as an example of a country where Western companies have had particular problems, but we don't know if it is the most difficult country.)

7 T (*What appears to be a barrier, however, can actually be a source of competitive advantage for those companies and managers ...* (lines 81–84); *This kind of cross-fertilisation has been taking place between Japanese and Western car-makers for decades, and has led to powerful innovations on both sides.* (lines 91–95))

B 1 Dutch

2 In the 1970s and 1980s

3 Because it was a large global company with a very strong corporate culture, which might override the local cultures where it operated. Hofstede set out to see if this was true or not.

4 Because in Spanish, *no va* means 'won't go'.

5 Because in Europe, there has been a tradition of luxury car-making, and customers have strong loyalty to local brands. In the US, the Lexus offered something different to domestic models.

6 They can reposition brands, and change the advertising or the product features to suit local sensitivities and expectations.

7 Firstly, because Chinese workers expect to be managed in a strong, authoritarian way, and even expect managers to help them with problems in their private lives. Secondly, there are language problems and different attitudes to ethics, reporting systems and workers' rights.

8 It can give companies extra advantages because of the exchange of ideas, which sometimes leads to innovations.

Vocabulary

A 1 b   2 a   3 a   4 b   5 a   6 a   7 b   8 b   9 b

B 1 overseas markets   2 to exploit   3 subsidiaries   4 poses   5 beliefs   6 values   7 preserve   8 loyalty
9 barriers   10 repositioning   11 establish   12 directive   13 to sort out   14 cross-fertilisation

C 1 subsidiaries   2 overseas   3 exploit   4 reposition   5 establish

Reading

A 1 Statement 2

B 1 Businesspeople have daily interaction at a distance with clients, business partners and colleagues from many other countries without the need to travel or live abroad.

2 They are run globally and around the clock, starting for example in Europe, then being handed over to the US, then to Asia and finally back to Europe.

3 There can be a big contrast in communication styles, cultures and expectations between people from different cultures.

4 They need to have employees with the right interpersonal and management skills.

5 Research into differences in personality traits between businesspeople from different countries.

6 They questioned nearly 7,500 managers and executives in more than 500 organisations across 12 countries

7 Emotional balance, extroversion, conscientiousness, agreeableness, and openness to new experiences.

8 The fact that agreeableness and emotional balance account for the biggest differences between managers and executives working across different countries.

9 Managers in the UK had among the lowest scores on agreeableness, and received only average scores in emotional balance. They scored high on extroversion.

10 Managers in Saudi Arabia and Japan are more concerned about maintaining group harmony, and seem more in touch with their emotions and feelings, but they are less inclined to speak openly.

11 Because UK managers may not put as much emphasis on group harmony, they may appear abrupt or non-caring to managers in Japan or Saudi Arabia.

12 Because managers in the UK and China score very differently on extroversion, activities such as brainstorming could be very unsuccessful with Chinese colleagues.

Vocabulary

A 1 1d 2c 3b 4e 5a

2 a) 3 b) 5 c) 2 d) 4 e) 2 f) 1 g) 3 h) 1 i) 5 j) 4

B 1 effort 2 abrupt; non-caring 3 interaction 4 expectations 5 interpersonal 6 Traits 7 inclined
8 come across 9 met with resistance 10 harmony

C 1 leaders (line 1) 2 colleagues (lines 2–3) 3 overseas (line 4) 4 clients (line 7) 5 vendors (line 7)
6 around-the-clock (lines 14–15) 7 executives (line 36) 8 organisations (line 37) 9 survey (line 38) 10 alone (line 86)

D 1 in 2 at 3 up 4 for 5 about 6 with 7 with 8 on 9 of

UNIT 3

Reading

A 1 c

2 To give a long explanation of the matter under discussion rather than express views directly.

3 By unanimous consent, with a lot of meetings before the meeting to make sure there are no surprises. Everyone has a chance to express their views and ideas.

B 1 Because a whiteboard is used during informal discussions and brainstorming with employees, which is not the way that Japanese executives work.

2 To express their views, to engage in brainstorming, to be a little less formal, to discuss the issues, to communicate openly and understandably (to a non-Japanese).

3 Because Japan has a very hierarchical culture. In business, this means that junior employees are not expected to speak in front of people more senior than them.

4 Because of the Japanese desire for unanimous consent and their need for careful and detailed planning; this means that everything takes a long time.

5 Consensus decision-making is where everyone can give their opinion about the issue, then a senior person takes the decision, which is then supported by everyone. Decision-making by unanimous consent is where everyone has to agree and one person can stop the decision. Federico Sacasa prefers consensus decision-making.

6 The Japanese are very process-oriented and often do things over and over again till they are right. Mr Sacasa believes in doing things right the first time.

7 They know it will be difficult to get the Japanese to change their working practices, but believe they will achieve it in the end.

Vocabulary

A 1a 2a 3b 4b 5b 6a 7a 8b 9a 10b 11b 12a 13b

B 1f 2d 3e 4b 5c 6a

C

Japanese style	Western style
give a long explanation formal, prefer presentations need for unanimous consent to make a decision meticulous planning focus on processes, lots of checking respect for each stage of the process	express ideas have a discussion of the issues and the logic consensus decision-making free, open expression communicate openly

UNIT 4

Reading

A 1 Statement c

2 To use just part of its US business model for the Chinese market at first, and to add other parts gradually as the market grew and became more established.

3 It has been very successful. Dell's market share grew by 60 per cent per year from 2000 to 2005, and is forecast to continue growing at twice the rate of the overall PC market.

B 1 When Marco Polo discovered that the Chinese used paper currency, he realised that it was unnecessary to bring coins from Europe. In the same way, foreign companies entering the Chinese market should bring only what is really needed and leave other parts of their Western business model behind.

2 1998

3 It allowed the company to use elements of its experience from the US without having to invent a new way of doing business for China.

4 The country's rules are often unpredictable.

5 Either importing its complete business model and trying to apply it in China, for which it is unlikely to be wholly suitable, or inventing a completely new business model, which means losing valuable experience from other markets.

6 Dell used a simpler form of their US model at first – they sold only desktop PCs to corporate customers.

7 They had to set up a system for payment on delivery, as credit cards were not widely used.

8 The biggest danger is importing a Western business model that is not adapted to the Chinese context and is too expensive to operate.

9 Foo Piau Phang

Vocabulary

A 1 a 2 a 3 b 4 a 5 b 6 b 7 b 8 a 9 b 10 b 11 b

B 1 capabilities 2 localise 3 unpredictable 4 core 5 incorporate 6 diminish 7 tenure
8 eligible 9 adjustments

C 1 f/g 2 a/c/h 3 e 4 f/g 5 i 6 d 7 a/c/h 8 b 9 a/c/h

UNIT 5

Reading

A 1 It is very large and it has sports and leisure facilities more common in a holiday resort.

2 It will be a hub for markets in South-East Asia and the Middle East.

3 To attract and keep the best employees it can.

B 1 $50m 2 14 acres 3 2007 4 1,000 5 10,000 6 $1.1bn 7 20 per cent 8 about 20
9 8 to 9 per cent 10 10 per cent or more 11 $750m 12 $100m 13 $150m

C 1 N (Only four are mentioned: cricket, basketball, aerobics and yoga.)

2 F (... *as Cisco's largest research-and-design centre outside the US is called* ... (lines 7–9))

3 T (*Although Cisco has low attrition rates of 8 to 9 per cent compared with double-digit rates at other companies* ... (lines 33–35))

4 F (*Cisco is betting on India as its eastern hemisphere hub, with Bangalore a short flight from the world's leading emerging markets in Asia and the Middle East.* (lines 48–52))

5 N (No figure is mentioned.)

Vocabulary

A 1 attrition 2 to replicate 3 to put the finishing touches to 4 to target 5 to base 6 to relocate
7 to shift 8 frivolous 9 amenities 10 to diversify 11 to hop 12 beachhead 13 to position yourself
14 hub 15 to retain

B 1 attrition 2 amenities; retain 3 beachhead 4 relocated 5 based 6 shift; replicate
7 diversifying; positioning 8 target 9 hop 10 hub 11 frivolous 12 putting the finishing touches to

C 1 to 2 in 3 in 4 into 5 on 6 to 7 to 8 of

D 1 largest 2 elegant 3 growing 4 state-of-the-art 5 low 6 retaining 7 frivolous 8 massive
9 cutting-edge 10 expansion

UNIT 6

Reading

A 1 Statement a

2 They have been invited by Schindler, which wants to demonstrate its latest elevators to show how modern and safe they are.

3 As far as we know, the accident is still being investigated by the police.

4 Because in their eyes, to apologise before they had investigated what caused the accident would have been an admission that the company was legally at fault.

5 Because a company in Japan has a social responsibility to the whole of society.

6 When doing business in a foreign culture, the local rules and customs may be different; and if you ignore them, it can be very expensive.

B 1 Because it has some of the latest elevators built by Schindler.

2 Switzerland

3 In 2006, in a Tokyo housing complex

4 It was carried out by two maintenance operators unconnected to Schindler.

5 They are taking legal action against Schindler and also against the two maintenance providers who serviced the elevator.

6 They did not cooperate with the local investigators, nor did they apologise for the accident.

7 Yes, the company has since apologised many times.

8 Mitsubishi Fuso is a truck maker owned by Daimler. Faulty parts on the trucks caused deaths and injuries in 2005. But the company apologised publicly, and the company President took flowers to a cemetery as part of this apology to show sympathy for the victims.

9 Because Schindler needs to re-establish its reputation in the social press before it can expect good treatment by the business and political press.

Vocabulary

A 1 b 2 a 3 b 4 a 5 b 6 a 7 a 8 b 9 b 10 b

B 1 state-of-the-art 2 leading 3 rebuild its image 4 malfunction 5 denies responsibility
6 legal action 7 social responsibility 8 model corporate citizen 9 reputation 10 pre-programmed

UNIT 7

Reading

A 1 F 2 T 3 T 4 F 5 T 6 T 7 F 8 T 9 T

B 1 To cut costs, increase profits and to benefit from another company's knowledge and expertise

2 91 per cent (*... only 9 per cent of mergers were judged 'completely successful'* ... (lines 9–11))

3 Mergers are not part of normal business; they are done under time pressure; and often the top executives making the decisions are biased in a particular direction.

4 A merger between two competitors with strong management teams, different working practices, different IT systems, etc.

5 She says that it is important to set clear targets, to manage a tight process and to take important decisions quickly. Also, the cultural difficulties should not be underestimated.

6 Small, very quick to take decisions or change direction (agile), not slowed down by strong processes or long-term planning.

7 Employees' morale will sink and people will leave the acquired organisation.

8 It did not try to change Scitex's way of working, as it recognised that it worked for Scitex and they should continue doing what they were good at.

9 Because all employees are expecting and prepared for change, a merger can be an opportunity to introduce new ways of working that neither set of employees may have accepted in the past.

10 If you want to know if a merger has been successful, you should measure the business value compared to what would have happened if the merger had not taken place.

Vocabulary

A 1 expertise 2 tight 3 slack 4 biased 5 economies of scale 6 leveraging 7 aligning
8 to underestimate 9 agile 10 alien 11 morale 12 hands-off 13 trickiest

B 1 cut 2 increase 3 fulfil 4 conduct 5 set 6 make/take 7 take over 8 establish 9 add 10 do

C 2 decisions 3 costs 4 objectives 5 goodwill 6 targets 7 a deal 8 value 9 profits 10 an organisation

D 2 added/improved value 3 reducing/cutting costs 4 increase/raise profits 5 doing/concluding; deal
6 create/establish; goodwill 7 meet/fulfil; objectives 8 set/fix; targets 9 make/take; decisions
10 taking over / acquiring an organisation

Over to you

1 1 b 2 c 3 a

2 **1 Volume extension**
   a) (Two of the world's biggest steel companies)
   d) (Based in different countries, these two global telecommunications manufacturers both operated worldwide; therefore this was a volume extension merger.)
   f) (Two hypermarket chains in France)
   g) (Despite being based in different countries, this was a volume extension merger rather than a regional one.)
   2 Regional extension
   b) (Two car manufacturers with strengths in different parts of the world, although with some overlap and scope for economies of scale through sharing of research and development, and purchasing)
   e) (Two car manufacturers operating in different parts of the world)
   h) (This was an acquisition by Wal-Mart of a German supermarket chain, in order to enter the German market.)
   3 Product extension
   c) Pepsi Co (drinks) and Quaker Oats (breakfast cereals)

3 **Successes (so far)**
   a) Arcelor and Mittal Steel
   b) Renault and Nissan
   c) Pepsi Co and Quaker Oats
   f) Carrefour and Promodes
   g) Air France and KLM
   Having difficulty
   d) Alcatel and Lucent (due to major cultural differences and poor integration, also unfortunate timing of market conditions)

Complete failures

e) Daimler and Chrysler (due to major cultural differences, both national and corporate)

h) Wertkauf and Wal-Mart (due to major cultural differences, both national and corporate)

UNIT 8

Reading

A 1 The German operations of Air Liquide and Messer Griesheim, which had been acquired by Air Liquide.

2 They brought in a consulting firm to help them deal with any problems immediately. A lot of workshops were organised, at which employees were asked to define new ways of working together.

3 Differences in corporate culture, especially different attitudes to risk.

4 The Dutch

B 1 Industrial gases

2 There were conflicting work styles, national cultural differences and fears about the future, especially job losses.

3 How to get people working together and at the same time to retain customers and not lose business.

4 A strong belief by both sides in their own superiority, a fear of job losses at Messer, and anxiety at Air Liquide that its flexible management style would be deadened by German 'rationality'.

5 Thirty-five employees were appointed to raise awareness of these 'viruses', to check if any 'viruses' appeared and to stop them spreading. They were also used as a discussion point in workshops attended by hundreds of employees.

6 The 'mental merger' project

7 For the first six months after the merger

8 Not according to Richard Schoenberg

9 He examined differences in management style in 129 UK acquisitions of continental European companies in the 1990s. He found that the only significant factor affecting performance was companies' attitude to risk: the bigger the difference between the bidder and target in their approach to risk, the less likely it was that the acquisition met its goals.

10 They are good at building bridges because they focus on the desired outcome of the merger rather than taking sides with different factions.

Vocabulary

A 1 b 2 a 3 a 4 b 5 b 6 a 7 a 8 a 9 b 10 b

B 1 d (v) 2 c (iv) 3 a (ii) 4 e (iii) 5 b (i)

C 1 resentment 2 conflicting 3 weaken 4 retain 5 superiority 6 flexible 7 fail 8 frequently 9 controversial

D 1 of working 2 in disrupting 3 before making 4 at building 5 from spreading 6 of discussing

UNIT 9

Reading

A 1 The merger integration had gone badly, and the cultural differences between the French and the Americans had become greater in the two years since the merger.

2 1 Richard Rawlinson 2 John Schwarz 3 Colette Hill

B 1 T (… *Ben Verwaayen, former Chief Executive of British Telecom* … (lines 2–3))

2 N (His nationality is not mentioned.)

3 N (This is not mentioned.)

4 F (*Before its acquisition by SAP, Business Objects was a French company with a strong US presence* … (lines 22–24))

5 T (*In the first six months after the acquisition, more than 35 per cent of senior managers transferred from SAP, while all of the original Business Objects corporate services people are now part of a global shared-services team.* (lines 31–36))

6 T (*Inevitably, some executives will go: more often than not, cultural changes mean people change.* (lines 57–60))

7 F (*The reason cultural problems matter is that they obstruct performance, and the need to improve performance is the best incentive to change culture. Besides, cultural change is easier when a company is challenged. This is the reason that such change had better start at the beginning of a turnaround.* (lines 62–69))

8 N (Although good communication after a merger is important, nothing is mentioned about hiring a PR company.)

9 T (*… pulling people together behind a common goal will be critical for success.* (lines 75–77))

10 T (*There will always be cultural differences across different parts of a global business. The problem here is that these have become public knowledge, potentially damaging Alcatel-Lucent's reputation.* (lines 82–87))

Vocabulary

A 1 mishandled 2 heightened 3 antipathy 4 head-on 5 drive 6 embrace 7 allies 8 obstruct
9 incentive 10 turnaround 11 lifeblood 12 collaborative 13 articulate 14 become public knowledge
15 reputation 16 stakeholder

B 1 a) mishandled integration b) cultural differences c) internal disagreements d) cross-border antipathy
2 a) Cultural sensitivity ...
b) ... combine the best of French passion and creativity with American drive and teamwork.
c) ... to appreciate the other people in the mix.
d) ... encourage cross-border, cross-functional teamwork ...
e) ... to embrace, not avoid, the strengths and differences of your global employees ...
3 a) ... pulling people together behind a common goal will be critical for success.
b) ... ensure a collaborative leadership team.
c) ... agree the corporate 'story' for the company, what it is and where it is going ...
d) ... articulate this vision to staff.
e) ... has agreed the direction of the company ...
f) ... create a communications plan (to keep each stakeholder in the business frequently and consistently informed about progress.)
g) ... create a common culture ...
h) ... making workers and the external audience aware of positive changes in the business.

C 1 1 cultural issues (lines 18–19) 2 cultural differences (lines 10–11) 3 cultural changes (line 59)
4 cultural sensitivity (line 21) 5 cultural problems (line 62)
2 *Suggested answers:* cultural identity, cultural diversity, cultural heritage, cultural misunderstanding, cultural awareness, cultural perspective, cultural challenge, cultural adjustment

D 1 on 2 from 3 on 4 for 5 into

UNIT 10

Reading

A 1 So they can gain international experience, especially of emerging markets in Asia, where the multinationals of the future will come from.
Because they will produce a bigger return in Asia.
It is considered an essential part of their career development.
2 Some employees are reluctant to go abroad at a time when they have new family responsibilities.
It is extremely expensive.
A significant number of employees leave their company soon after returning from an international assignment.

B 1 Two years
2 She will have learnt some Mandarin and will also have established a professional network in China.
3 PwC and HSBC
4 Because by the time they have the right professional skills, they also have family responsibilities.
5 That all its most promising young employees should go on international assignments to gain international experience.
6 No, it doesn't.
7 It could affect and harm their career prospects.
8 The cost can be three to four times their home-country salaries, plus lots of administrative support.
9 Fifteen per cent, and in some cases up to 40 per cent
10 Because they feel their experience abroad is not rewarded – they often come back to a similar position to the one they had before going abroad.
11 Companies need to make sure that employees returning from an international assignment move up the career ladder.

Vocabulary

A 1 b 2 a 3 a 4 b 5 b 6 b 7 a 8 b 9 b
B 1 secondment 2 posted 3 promising 4 hurdle 5 mismatch 6 drawback 7 mismanage
C 1 e 2 d 3 a 4 c 5 b
D 1 produce; return 2 gain; experience 3 recover their investment 4 feel at home 5 acquire skills
E 1 assignment
2 to second (/sə'kɒnd/ (stress on the last syllable)); compare with *second* (/'sekənd/), meaning 'between *first* and *third*' (stress on the first syllable)
3 to post
4 rising stars, high-flyers

UNIT 11

Reading

A 1 They are what are sometimes called 'global nomads' – the parents are from different countries and currently live in a third country; their three children were each born on a different continent.

2 Susan

3 Not very common (only 20 per cent find employment while abroad).

4 Family problems, including lack of career opportunities for the non-working partner

B 1 The number of overseas postings is increasing.

2 They want to build their own careers which they can continue in different countries.

3 They have moved five times to four cities (Sydney, New York, San Francisco, London) in three different countries (Australia, US, UK).

4 He is a business consultant and has succeeded in building a good career in each new location.

5 20 per cent

6 Few opportunities to work, culture shock, leaving friends and family, and the general stress of moving

7 Family concerns accounted for 89 per cent of refusals to go on overseas assignments, and spouse concerns accounted for 62 per cent of refusals. Family was also the reason for 28 per cent of early returns.

C 1 The maximum percentage of multinational corporate employees who are working abroad at any one time

2 The percentage of spouses who are employed before going on an expatriate assignment

3 The percentage of spouses who find employment while abroad

4 The percentage of overseas assignments refused because of family concerns

5 The percentage of overseas assignments refused because of spouse career concerns

6 The percentage of early returns due to family reasons

Vocabulary

A 1 allegiances 2 spouses 3 abroad 4 to settle 5 moves 6 lead-in times 7 thrived
8 trailing spouses 9 drive 10 peripatetic 11 culture shock 12 miserable 13 disastrous
14 concerns

B 1 c 2 f 3 d 4 b 5 e 6 a

C 1 overseas postings / expatriate assignments

2 Relocation companies

3 settle

4 home town

5 expatriate assignments / overseas postings

6 trailing spouse; miserable

7 culture shock

D 1 1 28 per cent 2 60 per cent 3 62 per cent 4 89 per cent 5 20 per cent 6 2 per cent
2 1 f 2 e 3 g 4 a 5 c 6 d 7 b

E 1 a 2 b 3 b 4 a 5 a

UNIT 12

Reading

A 1 How much time children spend outdoors
How much studying they do
Their opportunity to speak a foreign language
The cost of raising children
Whether a child is likely to remain in the country when he/she grows up

2 Spain, France, Germany and Canada (and India in an extra category)

3 The United Arab Emirates and the UK

4 He is the mayor of London. He wants to make London more attractive as a destination for expats and to secure the city's position 'as a top capital city'.

B 1 T (*Comparing results from 14 countries, ...* (line 5))

2 F (*The only place that does worse in the overall rankings for expat children is the United Arab Emirates.* (lines 8–11))

3 F (*HSBC's survey measures each country's suitability for expat offspring using five factors ...* (lines 12–14))

4 F (*The UK ranks below average in four of the categories.* (lines 28–29))

5 F (*'We're not going for the views of what children want, as it's their parents who are dragging them around the world.'* (lines 50–53))

6 N (No figures are given about this.)

7 N (No item is mentioned as being more important than any other.)

8 T (... *Spain, which tops the table as the best country for expat children.* (lines 64–66))
9 N (No one factor is mentioned as being more important than any other.)
10 N (They have the opportunity to learn Spanish, but we don't know how many do.)
11 T (... *with France scoring high on study time* ... (lines 74–75))

Vocabulary

A 1 c 2 a 3 g 4 e 5 i 6 f 7 b 8 h 9 d 10 j
B 1 best 2 well 3 better 4 above 5 high 6 top 7 comes bottom of 8 worst 9 Less/Fewer
   10 more expensive 11 before / ahead of 12 least
C 1 best; bring up 2 ranks 3 badly 4 tops 5 likelihood 6 overall 7 boost

---

UNIT 13

Reading

A 1 Very global. It is spread across six continents, from the US to Australia.
   2 Because they are spread across six continents and many time zones, some of the team have to wake up very early or stay at work very late when they have teleconferences.
   3 That only a third of virtual teams are successful in meeting their objectives.
   4 The most important thing is trust.
   5 To establish relationships within the team from the very beginning.
B 1 Six
   2 Once a week
   3 She has thought of splitting the team into hemispheres.
   4 Pros: the time-zone differences are not so big when they have teleconferences, and people aren't so tired. Cons: some people would have less contact with each other and might feel isolated.
   5 It is a geographically dispersed team that has to communicate through e-mail, telephone calls or video conferences rather than face to face.
   6 Because people rarely, if ever, see each other.
   7 To meet face to face when the team is formed and to take part in activities to get to know each other.
   8 It includes practical things, such as responding to e-mails within a fixed time, as well as the importance of psychological support, which could include sending encouraging messages and acknowledging the efforts of others.
   9 Team leaders should help to build relationships by trying to get people to share some level of social information, for example about their country or their family.
   10 They should summarise relevant information from conversations with individual members of the team for the rest of the group, but not overwhelm people with too much information.

Vocabulary

A 1 isolated 2 geographically dispersed 3 crucial 4 in line with 5 face-to-face 6 code of practice
   7 Consistency 8 social information 9 fine line 10 inundating
B 1 e/f 2 c 3 f/e 4 a 5 b 6 d
C 1 wide awake 2 late in the evening 3 rarely 4 build 5 short-term 6 acknowledging 7 success
D 1 d (iii) 2 e (v) 3 b (i) 4 c (iv) 5 a (ii)
E 1 draw up 2 put in 3 kick off 4 set out 5 come about

UNIT 14

Reading

A 1 Germany
   2 Because it is located in Saarland, the German state near the French border that has changed from French to German rule several times over the centuries.
   3 The Germans are good at practical work and the French are better at theory.
   4 The title is a combination of two metaphors. When people from different cultures are thrown together, this is known as a 'a melting pot'. Dillinger Hütte is a steel company, and 'forging' is part of the steel-making process, meaning 'making something by melting it at a very high temperature'.
B 1 Paul Belche uses making mayonnaise as a metaphor to describe how the mix of cultures in his steel plant works well, but it would also be easy to get it wrong.
   2 Specialist steels for applications such as oil pipelines
   3 5,500
   4 10 per cent are French speakers, 90 per cent German speakers
   5 Neither. He is from Luxembourg.

6 The French speakers are better because they work harder at it.
7 Lunch follows a French approach, with a later finishing time than is normal in Germany.
8 The company invites customers to tour the steel plant and also to attend scientific seminars.
9 It is difficult – the article says it is a 'tough business'.
10 The mix of cultures and different cultural characteristics
11 A soufflé (... *the mix of cultures [...] provides a soufflé of experiences* ... (lines 76–77))

Vocabulary

A 1 culinary   2 to coax   3 tactics   4 sovereignty   5 poses   6 to link   7 to tour   8 hands-on
9 tough

B 1 tour   2 tough   3 tactics   4 hands-on   5 coax   6 linking   7 sovereignty

C 1 1 explanation   2 mix/mixture   3 production/product   4 management/manager   5 recognition
6 encouragement   7 announcement   8 development/developer   9 demonstration   10 solution
11 provision   12 invitation
2 1 lead   2 theorise   3 weaken   4 strengthen   5 sell   6 succeed

D 1 to   2 with   3 at   4 of   5 from   6 at   7 with   8 to   9 on   10 out of   11 between   12 out of

Over to you

2 1 police   2 cooks   3 engineers   4 organisers   5 lovers   6 cooks   7 engineers   8 police
9 lovers   10 organisers

UNIT 15

Reading

A 1 c
2 All partners need to be aiming at the same goal and to share the same vision; each partner needs to recognise exactly what they are contributing to the project; finally the group needs to have a clear system and effective communication tools for working together – for making decisions, having discussions, exchanging information, etc.

B 1 F (*Mr Cain is an executive board member of* [...] *a multi-disciplinary research collaboration between academic research organisations and companies from the UK, France, Germany, Switzerland, Italy, Latvia, Spain, Denmark and Slovenia.* (lines 18–26)) (The group is European, not global.)
2 T (... *a multi-disciplinary research collaboration* ... (lines 21–22))
3 N (They come from both universities and businesses, but we are not told anything about the numbers from each category.)
4 T (*The fact that the partnership is progressing well and is on target to achieve its aims is partly because all partners are aiming at the same goal.* (lines 33–37))
5 N (The article states that it is important that they know their roles, but nothing is mentioned specifically about this.)
6 T (*Decision-making in a large collaborative project can be difficult* [...] *If you are so democratic that you are taking referendums all the time, things take a very long time to change.* (lines 52–56))
7 T (*Face-to-face meetings take place quarterly – or once a month during important phases of a project – and are reserved for taking decisions.* (lines 60–64))
8 N (Part of the work is done that way, but we are not told how much.)
9 F (*It is not necessary for two organisations to have identical approaches or identical cultures: indeed, if they did, it would limit the opportunity for each to benefit from the other's expertise.* (lines 74–79))

Vocabulary

A 1 b   2 a   3 a   4 b   5 b   6 a   7 b   8 a
B 1 of succeeding   2 by organising   3 for exchanging and sharing   4 of working
C 1 b (iii)   2 d (v)   3 e (i)   4 f (vi)   5 a (iv)   6 c (ii)
D 1 harmonious   2 inevitably   3 succeeding   4 large-scale   5 speed up   6 strengths   7 identical   8 limit

UNIT 16

Reading

A 1 In Mysore, India
2 To ensure that their graduates will be able to work comfortably as part of an international, diverse workforce.
3 They will receive technical training, while at the same time learning about the countries and communities around the world that they will ultimately operate in.

B 1 F (*'If you visit a workplace in the UK, you'll generally find people approaching their daily tasks individually. If you visit a workplace in India, on the other hand, you'll find people are much more happy to multitask ...'* (lines 1–6))

Glossary

A

abroad *adj.* in or to a foreign country

abrupt *adj.* seeming rude and unfriendly, especially because you do not waste time in friendly conversation

add value *v.* to create an increase in the value of something after working on it, such as after a merger

address (problems) *v.* to try to deal with (problems)

adjustment *n.* a change that is made to something in order to correct or improve it

admission *n.* a statement accepting that something bad is true, or that you have done something wrong

agile *adj.* able to move quickly and easily

agreeableness *n.* getting on well with other people

alien *adj.* not familiar, very strange

align *v.* to organise or change something so that it has the right relationship to something else

allegiance *n.* loyalty to a country, belief, etc.

ally *n.* someone who helps and supports you, especially against people who are trying to cause problems for you

amenities *n.pl.* things that make it comfortable or enjoyable to live or work somewhere

anti-climax *n.* something that is not as exciting as you expected it to be

antipathy *n.* a feeling of strong dislike towards someone or something

apparent *adj.* seems to have happened, although it has not been proved

applicant *n.* a person who applies for a job

appreciation *n.* the ability to understand a situation and know why it is important or serious

around-the-clock *adj.* 24 hours a day

artefact *n.* an object such as a tool or decoration, especially one that is of cultural and historical interest

articulate *v.* to use words effectively to express your ideas

assignment *n.* when someone is sent to work in a particular place

assimilation *n.* the process of becoming an accepted part of a group

assume *v.* to believe that something is true, even though you cannot be certain

assumptions *n.pl.* things that you think are true, even though you cannot be certain

attitudes *n.pl.* the opinions and feelings that you usually have about something

attrition rate *n.* the rate at which employees leave a company

awareness *n.* knowledge or understanding of a particular subject, situation, or thing

B

base *v.* to have somewhere as the main place from which a company or organisation controls its activities

beachhead *n.* a strategic position from where you can advance further

behaviour *n.* the way that someone acts in different situations

beliefs *n.pl.* ideas that you believe to be true, especially ones that form part of a system of ideas

best practices *n.pl.* good examples of how something should be done

biased *adj.* unfairly preferring one person or group over another

board member *n.* one of the group of people chosen by shareholders to control a company and decide its policies

boost *v.* to help something to increase or improve

brainstorming *n.* a way of developing new ideas and solving problems in which people suggest lots of ideas and the best ones are chosen

brand-new *adj.* new and not yet used

breeding ground *n.* a place where problems can develop easily

bring up *v.* to look after a child until he/she becomes an adult

build a team *v.* to make a group work well together as a team

build relationships *v.* to create a good way of working together

build trust *v.* to create a belief in the honesty and goodness of someone

C

candidate *n.* someone who is being considered for a job

cap *v.* to put a limit on something

capabilities *n.pl.* natural abilities, skills or power that make a person or organisation able to do something, especially something difficult

carry out *v.* to do a particular piece of work, such as a survey

cement *v.* to make a relationship stronger

coax *v.* to gently persuade someone to do something

code of practice *n.* a set of rules about how people should behave

cohort *n.* a group of people of the same age, social class, etc.

cold *adj.* unfriendly or lacking normal human feelings such as sympathy, pity, humour, etc.

collaborate *v.* to work with another person, company or organisation to achieve something

collaboration *n.* the activity of working together with another person, company, etc. in order to achieve something

collaborative *adj.* A *collaborative* project involves two or more people, companies, etc. working together in order to achieve something.

collapse *v.* If a company, organisation or system *collapses*, it suddenly fails or becomes too weak to continue.

colleagues *n.pl.* people you work with, used especially by professional people or managers

come about *v.* to happen, especially in a way that is not planned

come across *v.* to make someone have a particular opinion of you when they meet you

come bottom *v.* to be in last place in a survey or competition

come top *v.* to be in first place in a survey or competition

common culture *n.* a culture shared by everyone

common goal *n.* an aim or objective which everyone accepts

competitive advantage *n.* an advantage that makes a company more able to succeed in competing with others

concerns *n.pl.* things that worry you

conclude a deal *v.* to reach an agreement

conduct *v.* to carry out an activity or process in order to obtain information or prove facts

conflicting *adj. Conflicting* ideas, beliefs or opinions are different from each other and cannot both be true.

conscientiousness *n.* tendency to be reliable, well organised, self-disciplined and careful

consensus *n.* agreement among all the people involved

consistency *n.* the ability to remain the same in behaviour and attitudes

controversial *adj.* causing strong feelings of disagreement

convey a message *v.* to communicate ideas or information

cope with *v.* to deal successfully with a particular situation

core *adj.* most important or most basic

corporate culture *n.* the attitudes or beliefs that are shared in a particular organisation

criss-cross the world *v.* to go to many different countries

critical *adj.* Something that is *critical* is very important because what happens in the future depends on it.

cross-border *adj.* something that involves organisations in two or more countries

cross-fertilisation *n.* the mixing of the ideas, customs, etc. of different groups of people, to benefit all

cross-functional *adj.* something that involves people in different job areas

crucial *adj.* Something that is *crucial* is extremely important, because everything else depends on it.

cues *n.pl.* using someone else's actions or behaviour to show you what you should do or how you should behave

culinary *adj.* relating to cooking

cultural barriers *n.pl.* see **cultural differences**

cultural convergence *n.* when different cultures come closer together

cultural differences *n.pl.* differences between cultures which can make communication and working together more difficult

cultural divides *n.pl.* see **cultural differences**

cultural mix *n.* when people from different cultures mix together

cultural perspectives *n.pl.* the way people of a particular culture think about something

cultural sensitivity *n.* the quality of understanding how people from another culture feel and being careful not to offend them

culture clashes *n.pl.* differences between cultures which lead to misunderstandings and disagreements

culture shock *n.* the feeling of being confused or anxious that you get when you visit a foreign country or a place that is very different from the one you are used to

customisation *n.* changing the way that something works so it is exactly what you want or need

D

deal *n.* agreement or arrangement, especially one that involves the sale of something

decision-making process *n.* the way in which decisions are taken

decisive *adj.* good at making decisions quickly and with confidence

deny *v.* to say that something is not true, or that you do not believe something

devise *v.* to invent a method of doing something

diminish *v.* to make something become smaller or less

dip their toes *v.* to do something for the first time or to try something cautiously

direct *adj.* saying exactly what you mean in an honest, clear way

directive *adj.* giving instructions and clear directions

disastrous *adj.* very bad or ending in failure

disrupt *v.* to prevent a situation, event, system, etc. from working in the normal way

diverse *adj.* very different from each other

diversify *v.* to develop additional products or activities

diversity *n.* the fact that very different people or things exist within a group or place

domestic *adj.* relating to the country you live in, rather than abroad

draw up *v.* to prepare a written document, such as a list or contract

drawback *n.* a disadvantage of a situation, product, etc. that makes it less attractive

dress *n.* the type of clothes that are typical of a particular place, time in history, etc.

drive *n.* the energy and determination that makes you try hard to achieve something

due diligence *n.* when a company thinking of buying another looks carefully at its accounts, as it must do by law before the deal can be agreed

E

economies of scale *n.pl.* the fact that as the amount of goods or services produced increases, the cost per unit decreases

eligible *adj.* allowed to do something or receive something

embrace *v.* to eagerly accept a new idea, opinion, religion, etc.

emergence *n.* when something begins to be known or noticed

emotional balance *n.* tendency to be calm, relaxed and secure in yourself

eventually *adv.* after a long time, or after a lot of things have happened

expatriate *n.* someone who has moved to a foreign country to live and work

expectations *n.pl.* the belief that something will happen

expertise *n.* special skills or knowledge in an area of work or study

explicit *adj.* expressed in a way that is very clear and direct

extroversion *n.* being confident and liking social interaction

eye-opener *n.* an experience from which you learn something surprising or new

F

face issues *v.* to deal with problems

face-to-face *adj.* involving two people who are together in the same place

far-reaching *adj.* having a great influence or effect

feel at home *v.* to feel relaxed and comfortable in a particular place or situation

figure out *v.* to understand something or to solve a problem

fine line *n.* If there is a *fine line* between two things, they are almost the same as each other.

fix targets *v.* to give people something to aim at

flexible *adj.* able to make changes or deal with a situation that is changing

focus on processes *v.* to concentrate on the step-by-step way of doing something

force-fit *v.* to make something be the right size to go somewhere

foresee *v.* to think or know that something is going to happen in the future; to predict

formal *adj.* suitable for serious situations or occasions

fresh *adj.* having just finished your education or training, and not having a lot of experience

frivolous *adj.* lacking any real purpose; not serious or sensible

fulfil aims *v.* to reach a target or goal that has been set

G

gain experience *v.* to learn more about a job over a period of time

geographically dispersed *adj.* working in different countries, often far apart

get at *v.* to try to suggest something without saying it directly

get through *v.* to succeed in making someone understand something, especially when this is difficult

global competition *n.* competition between companies from different countries

global demand *n.* total demand from all over the world

global economy *n.* the economy of the world seen as a whole

global footprint *n.* having offices and activities in many parts of the world

global interdependence *n.* the degree to which countries around the world are connected and need each other

global team *n.* a team of people based in different countries around the world

goodwill *n.* a feeling of wanting to be friendly and helpful to someone

ground-breaking *adj.* *Ground-breaking* work involves making new discoveries, using new methods, etc.

guilt *n.* the fact that you have broken an official law or moral rule

H

hands-off *adj.* not telling the people you are in charge of exactly what to do, but letting them make their own decisions

hands-on *adj.* doing something yourself rather than just talking about it or telling other people to do it

harmonious *adj.* combining well with each other

harmony *n.* a situation in which people live or work together without disagreeing with each other

head-on *adv.* If someone deals with a problem *head-on*, they do not try to avoid it, but deal with it in a direct and determined way.

heighten *v.* If something *heightens* a feeling or emotion, or if a feeling or emotion *heightens*, it becomes stronger or increases.

hierarchical *adj.* an organisation or structure in which the staff are organised in levels and the people at one level have authority over those below them

high-flyer *n.* someone in a company who is talented and who will be promoted quickly through the organisation

hire *v.* to agree to give someone a job

home town *n.* the place where you were born and spent your childhood

hop *v.* to move somewhere quickly or suddenly

hub *n.* a city or country where there is a lot of business activity because it is central in relation to other places, there are good communications, etc.

humble *adj.* not proud and not thinking you are better than others

hurdle *n.* a problem or difficulty that you must deal with before you can achieve something

I

idiosyncrasies *n.pl.* unusual or strange ways of doing things

immerse *v.* to become completely involved in an activity

implement *v.* to take action or make changes that you have officially decided should happen

implicit *adj.* suggested or understood without being stated directly

incentive *n.* something which is used to encourage people to do something, especially to make them work harder or produce more

incorporate *v.* to include or add something to a group, system, plan, etc.

indirect *adj.* not saying something in a clear, definite way

informal *adj.* relaxed and friendly without being restricted by rules of correct behaviour

integration *n.* the combining of two or more organisations, activities, etc. so that they become more effective, make better profits, etc.

interaction *n.* the activity of talking to other people, working together with them, etc.

interpersonal *adj.* relating to relationships between people

inundated *adj.* receiving so much of something that you cannot easily deal with it all

isolated *adj.* feeling alone and unhappy, with no friends

J

joint venture *n.* a business activity in which two or more companies have invested together

jump on the bandwagon *v.* to follow an idea or activity that suddenly becomes very popular

jump to conclusions *v.* to make a decision about something before you have all the facts

K

kick off *v.* If you *kick off* a discussion, meeting, event, etc., you start it.

knowledgeable *adj.* knowing a lot

kudos *n.* the state of being admired and respected for being important or for doing something important

L

lead-in time *n.* the time needed for preparation

leading *adj.* best, most important, most successful

learning curve *n.* the rate at which you learn a new skill

legal action *n.* the act of using the legal system to settle a disagreement, etc.

leveraging *n.* getting as much advantage or profit as possible from something

lifeblood *n.* the thing that keeps something strong and healthy and allows it to continue successfully

likelihood *n.* the degree to which something can reasonably be expected to happen

link *v.* to connect two things together

local sensitivities *n.pl.* the way people in a specific place feel about something

localise *n.* to organise a business or industry so that things happen at a local level rather than a national one

M

malfunction *n.* a fault in the way a machine works

management style *n.* the way in which an organisation is run by its top managers

market saturation *n.* when everyone in a particular market has already bought the product a company offers

master the basics *v.* to understand and learn the most important aspects or principles of something

meet with resistance *v.* to be in a situation where people refuse to do what you want them to do

meticulous *adj.* very careful about small details, always making sure that everything is done correctly

mirror *v.* to match the qualities or features of someone else

miserable *adj.* extremely unhappy, for example because you feel lonely

mishandled *adj.* when a situation is dealt with badly, because of a lack of skill or care

mishandled integration *n.* when a merger between two organisations is badly handled

misjudgement *n.* forming a wrong opinion about a person or a situation

mismanage *v.* to manage something badly

mismatch *n.* a combination of things or people that do not work well together or are not suitable for each other

misunderstanding *n.* a problem caused by not understanding someone or something correctly

mitigate *v.* to make a situation or the effects of something less harmful or serious

model corporate citizen *n.* when a company shows itself to be a good member of the society in which it operates

morale *n.* the level of confidence and positive feelings among a group of people who work together

move *n.* going to live or work in a different place

multitask *v.* to do several things at the same time

mutual trust *n.* when two or more people or groups have confidence in each other

N

niche *n.* a job or activity that is very suitable for you

non-caring *adj.* not concerned about other people

norms *n.pl.* standards of behaviour that are accepted in a particular society

O

obstruct *v.* to prevent something from happening, by making it difficult

offspring *n.* someone's child or children – often used humorously

on target *adj.* working well towards what you are trying to achieve

open expression *n.* speaking freely and saying what you really think in a discussion

open-minded *adj.* willing to consider and accept other people's ideas and opinions

openness to new experiences *n.* being ready and prepared to try new things

operate *v.* to do business (in a particular country)

organisational culture *n.* the attitudes and beliefs shared by everyone who works in a particular organisation

overall *adj.* considering or including everything

overseas *adv.* to, in, or from a foreign country

P

peer *n.* someone who is the same age or has the same job, social position, etc. as the person you are talking about

perceptive *adj.* Someone who is *perceptive* notices things quickly and understands situations, people's feelings, etc. well.

peripatetic *adj.* travelling from place to place, especially in order to do your job

perspective *n.* a way of thinking about or looking at something

pitfall *n.* a problem or difficulty that is likely to happen in a particular job, course of action or activity

play to your strengths *v.* to concentrate on the things which you are good at

pose *v.* to ask a question, especially one that needs to be carefully thought about

position yourself *v.* to put yourself in the right place (for future opportunities)

post *n.* a job, especially an important or well-paid one

posting *n.* an occasion when an employee is sent to another country by his/her employer to do a particular job

post-merger performance *n.* how two companies perform after a merger

pre-programmed *adj.* given a set of instructions to act in a certain way in the future

prerequisite *n.* something that is necessary before something else can happen or be done

produce a return *v.* to get profit or income from time or money invested

promising *adj.* showing signs of being successful or good in the future

public knowledge *n.* something that is known by everyone

public opinion *n.* the opinions or beliefs that ordinary people have about a particular subject

put in *v.* to spend time or effort doing something

R

raise *v.* to bring up (a child)

rank *v.* to decide the position of something in a list in order of quality or importance

ranking *n.* the position of something or someone in a list that has been arranged in order of quality or importance

rebuild *v.* to improve a situation so that it is as good as it was in the past

recover your investment *v.* to get back money or another result according to what you have spent

recruit *v.* to find new people to work for an organisation, do a job, etc.

redemption *n.* being forgiven for having done something bad

reduce costs *v.* to spend less money on running a business

relocate *v.* If a company or worker *relocates* or is *relocated*, he/she moves to a different place.

relocation company *n.* a company that specialises in helping executives and their families move to live and work in another country

remorse *n.* a strong feeling of being sorry that you have done something very bad

repair *v.* to try to remove the damage a mistake or wrong action has caused

replicate *v.* to do or make something again in the same way as before

repugnant *adj.* very unpleasant and offensive

reputation *n.* the opinion people have about how good or bad someone or something is

resentment *n.* a feeling of anger because something has happened that you think is unfair

responsibility *n.* blame for something bad that has happened

retain *v.* to keep someone or something, such as staff, customers, etc.

rigid *adj.* *Rigid* methods, systems, etc. are very strict and difficult to change.

ritual purification *n.* showing in a very public way that you are sorry for past actions and seek society's forgiveness

rising stars *n.pl.* people in an organisation who are talented and are likely to reach high positions

rotate *v.* If people *rotate* jobs, they do the jobs for a fixed period of time, one after the other.

S

second *v.* to send an employee to work for another organisation for a period of time

secondment *n.* arranging for an employee to work for another organisation for a period of time

self-knowledge *n.* an understanding of your own character and behaviour

set out *v.* to write about something, such as a group of facts, ideas or reasons, in an organised way

set targets *v.* to give people something to aim at

setting *n.* the place where something is or where something happens; the general environment

settle *v.* to go to live permanently in a particular place

shift *v.* to move something from one place to another

slack *n.* extra time or resources in a project, which can be used if needed

small-scale *adj.* involving only a small number of things or a small area

social responsibility *n.* the duties and role a company has towards society in general

sovereignty *n.* the right to rule a country

spell *n.* a short period of time

spouse *n.* a husband or wife

spread your wings *v.* to start activities in different areas or parts of the world

staff *v.* to provide the workers for an organisation

stakeholder *n.* a person or group that is involved in and can be affected by a particular organisation, e.g. employees, shareholders

stand out *v.* to be much better than other similar people or things

state-of-the-art *adj.* the most modern and recently developed methods, materials or knowledge

stereotype *n.* a belief or idea (often unfair or untrue) of what a particular type of person or thing is like

stumble *v.* to stop or make a mistake when you are speaking

subordinate *n.* someone less important or powerful than someone else; a more junior person

succinctly *adv.* clearly expressed in a few words

suffer *v.* to experience something very unpleasant

superiority *n.* an attitude that shows you think you are better than other people

support *v.* to show you agree with a person or group of people, or their ideas, plans, etc.

swift *adj.* quick, fast

T

tackle *v.* to deal with a problem

tactics *n.pl.* a method or plan to achieve something

take at face value *v.* to accept something without thinking if it is true or not

take someone down a few notches *v.* to make someone feel a bit less confident about him or herself

target *v.* to aim products at a particular area or group of people

team charter *n.* an agreement or contract by all members of a team on how they will work together

teamwork *n.* the ability of a group of people to work well together

tenure *n.* the period of time when someone has an important job or position

thrive *v.* to become very successful

tight timeframe *n.* when the time available to do something is very limited

top *v.* to be higher than all the others

tough *adj.* difficult to do or deal with

traditions *n.pl.* beliefs, customs or ways of doing something that have existed for a long time, or these beliefs, customs, etc. in general

trailing spouse *n.* wife, husband or partner who accompanies an executive on a foreign assignment

trait *n.* a particular quality in someone's character

transparency *n.* when rules, methods, or business dealings are clear and people can see that they are fair and honest

tricky *adj.* difficult to do or difficult to deal with

turnaround *n.* a situation in which something changes from bad to good

U

ultimately *adv.* finally, after everything else has been done or considered

unanimous *adj.* A *unanimous* decision or statement is one that everyone agrees with.

underestimate *v.* to think that something is smaller or less difficult than it really is

undermine *v.* to gradually make someone or something less strong or effective

unique selling point *n.* a feature of a product or service that makes it different from all others (also *unique selling proposition*)

unpredictable *adj.* changing a lot so it is impossible to know what will happen

unthinkable *adj.* something that is impossible to accept or imagine

uproot *v.* to force someone to leave the place where they live

V

values *n.pl.* the principles and beliefs that influence the behaviour and way of life of a particular group or community

vendor *n.* a company or person that sells something; also known as *supplier* in a business context

virtual team *n.* a team that is based in different locations, usually different countries, who communicate mainly by phone, conference calls, e-mails, etc.

vital *adj.* extremely important and necessary

voice *v.* to express your feelings or thoughts

W

weaken *v.* to make something less powerful or successful

well-travelled *adj.* a person who has travelled to many countries

well-proven *adj.* something that has been shown to be effective before

wide awake *adj.* not sleeping and very alert

work experience *n.* a short period of time during which a young person works for a company in order to learn about a job and about working life in general

work out *v.* to find an answer to a problem or a way of dealing with a situation

work permit *n.* an official document that allows someone to work in another country, usually for a specific length of time

work placement *n.* when a student spends time in an organisation to gain work experience

work styles *n.pl.* the ways in which people work in an organisation

workforce *n.* all the people who work in a particular country, industry or factory

workload *n.* the amount of work that a person or organisation has to do

workplace *n.* the room or building where you work